ALSO BY DENIS DONOVAN AND
DEBORAH MCINTYRE

Healing the Hurt Child

What Did I Just Say!?!

Denis Donovan, M.D., M.Ed.

Deborah McIntyre, M.A., R.N.

What Did I Just Say!?!

How New Insights
into Childhood Thinking
Can Help You Communicate
More Effectively with
Your Child

Henry Holt and Company   New York

Henry Holt and Company, LLC
Publishers since 1866
115 West 18th Street
New York, New York 10011

Henry Holt® is a registered trademark of
Henry Holt and Company, LLC.

Copyright © 1999 by Denis Donovan and Deborah McIntyre
All rights reserved.
Published in Canada by Fitzhenry & Whiteside Ltd.,
195 Allstate Parkway, Markham, Ontario L3R 4T8.

Library of Congress Cataloging-in-Publication Data
Donovan, Denis
What did I just say!?! : how new insights into childhood
thinking can help you communicate more effectively with
your child / Denis Donovan, Deborah McIntyre.—1st ed.
p.   cm.
Includes bibliographical references and index.
ISBN 0-8050-6079-0 (alk. paper)
1. Interpersonal communication in children—United States.
2. Communication in the family—United States.
3. Parent and child—United States.   I. McIntyre, Deborah.
II. Title.
BF723.C57D66   1999   99-11987
649'.1—dc21   CIP

Henry Holt books are available for special promotions and
premiums. For details contact: *Director, Special Markets*.

First Edition 1999

Designed by Kate Nichols

Printed in the United States of America
All first editions are printed on acid-free paper. ∞

1   3   5   7   9   10   8   6   4   2

for

Anne Sullivan

who has always understood

what we've been saying

and

who never gave up hoping

that Denis would say it better

Contents

What Did I Just Say!?!

1

"What Did I Just Say!?!"

In a toy store, we come across a mother and her four-year-old, who is pushing boxes of toy cars and trucks around on a shelf, trying to see what's behind them. The mother looks sternly at her son, clearly wanting him to leave the boxes alone. When he doesn't stop, the mother says, "Do you want a spanking?" and her son, who looked up momentarily, continues his search for something on the shelf.

"DO YOU WANT A SPANKING?" the mother repeats, this time much more sternly and stressing every single word. When the boy doesn't stop touching the store items, the mother walks over and whacks him hard on the rear, causing him to arch like a bow and trip down the aisle. No sooner does he stop moving than he again begins to forage through the toys on the shelf. As we move out of earshot, we hear the mother shout, "WHAT DID I JUST SAY!?!"

Many parents today will tell you that they're not getting what they want from their children. Parents have to struggle to get the respect, cooperation, affection, acceptable behavior, completed tasks, and academic achievement they consider appropriate. Quite a few parents have actually thrown in the towel. After all, these problems not only seem to plague the whole country, they appear to be taking on epidemic proportions. And there's very little indication that things are likely to get better.

Almost no one's satisfied or optimistic about the future: parents, educators, mental health professionals, or the media.

By contrast, the outlook of this book is surprisingly upbeat. That's because we believe that parents can discover in their own homes what we have discovered over many years of clinical work with children and families—namely, that many frustrating and seemingly insurmountable problems actually have simple, easy to understand causes, as well as equally simple and easy to understand solutions.

More often than not, the problems are a matter of simple—but pervasive—miscommunication. The solutions lie in two fundamental avenues: in becoming aware of what we actually say when we speak to our kids, and in beginning to understand children more on their own terms, as they actually are.

Sound too good to be true? Our years of experience say otherwise. Read on, and you will see how problems that have been diagnosed as oppositional-defiant behavior, refusal to take responsibility for one's actions, academic underachievement, and even formal psychiatric disorders such as Attention Deficit–Hyperactivity Disorder (ADHD or ADD), Learning Disabilities (LD), Separation Anxiety Disorder (SAD), depression, and anxiety have yielded to little more than a bit of patience and a willingness to see old things in a new way.

Consider our story from the toy store.

When parents like this harried mother of a four-year-old encounter what they consider uncooperative behavior, they often expect the worst. Some lose control in frustration. Others reach for labels, diagnostic pigeonholes all too eagerly handed out by mental health professionals. Is this child *oppositional* and *defiant*, or is there a *receptive language disorder*?

But what really happened in the toy store?

What's really going on is a huge communication mismatch, and an absolutely unnecessary one. When the mom asked her four-year-old whether he wanted a spanking, we assume that what she really meant was "Don't touch" or "Leave those toys alone." But that's not at all what she said. Instead, she asked her son a question: "Do you want a spanking?" So, even if she had wanted her son to think about "being good," "doing as you're told," or, presumably, "not touching the toys," this mother in fact *changed the subject* to whether her son wanted a spanking. As we walked away, what we heard was still not a clear and unequivocal command that

her son not touch the toys. Instead, her loud and exasperated words were, "What did I just say?"

The question, of course, doesn't have a thing to do with whether or not her son should touch items on store shelves. So the question is self-defeating. If you want an answer, ask a question. If you want action, issue a command—in this case, "Don't touch the toys."

We All Do It

It's not just moms who often don't hear what they're really saying to their children. Doctors, teachers, therapists—unless they're really tuned in to this issue—all have a tendency to say things that are very different from what they really mean and what they really want to communicate. And kids, as we'll explain later, have "logic antennas"—they tune into what parents and other adults say literally and logically.

When Calvin says to his mom, "Weren't you listening either?" he sounds like a disrespectful smart aleck—which, of course, much of the time he is. But Calvin does have a point here. Beneath his flippant attitude is much more than a mere technicality. Rarely do parents, or adults in general, hear what they're really saying.

Shortly after running into the mom and her four-year-old at Toys "Я" Us, we happen upon a similar scene in a grocery store. Looking for the produce section in a large supermarket, we run into a bottleneck where a group of grandmotherly women are admiring an extremely handsome and compact little Robert Redford lookalike dressed shirtless in Oshkosh B'Gosh coveralls.

"He is *such* a cutie," one woman exclaims.

"And he's *so* well behaved!" says another.

"He looks *just* like his dad," adds a third. "How old is he?" The obviously proud young father, another Robert Redford lookalike dressed Florida-style in running shorts and a Gold's Gym T-shirt, plays his role as matter-of-fact successful parent.

"Two and a half," says the dad, adding, "he's a good minder."

We're just about through the checkout line when we again come upon the father and son. The dad heads right from the checkout counter toward the packaged ice refrigerator by the exit, while Junior, who hadn't noticed his dad's detour, continues straight toward the automatic doors.

"If you go by that street, you're in trouble!" says the dad firmly. Struck by an acute attack of parent-deafness, Junior picks up speed, his waddle-run carrying him to within a few feet of the very busy strip mall parking, where his dad grabs him by one arm and pulls him back.

"Now WHAT DID I JUST SAY!?!" we hear once again as the pair disappear back into the store.

It's Everywhere!

If you take the trouble to look and listen carefully, you'll discover that scenes like those we encountered in the mall and the grocery store are by no means rare. In fact, you'll run into such scenes repeatedly wherever you find parents and children. The more you pay attention to these things, the more the blur of the obvious will give way to surprising details, details that you've always seen but never really appreciated.

As you watch and listen to what's going on around you, ask yourself a simple question. *Is that parent—or crossing guard, PE teacher, or camp counselor—getting what he or she wants?* Much of the time the answer will be NO. Then ask yourself what all those ineffectual words have in common with "What did I just say!?!" You'll discover that such expressions are *empty* because they don't really communicate anything relevant to the intentions of the speaker. The more you listen, the more you'll hear empty utterances that lead nowhere.

- Can't you behave?
- Are you going to stop it?

- Billy, what's going on? (As Billy screams his head off)
- You're driving me crazy.
- It's not nice to hit Daddy.
- We're not a hitting family.
- We don't do that.
- That's not polite.

Let's take a look at these very common expressions and see what's going on.

"Can't you behave?" is, first and foremost, a question. So we already know what will pass instantaneously through the child's mind—the answer: "Sure, I can, if I want to. But I don't want to."

"Can't you behave?" is also a suggestion. To see whether a question is a suggestion or a command, just make it a statement. In this case, we get "You can't behave." So the very form of the question suggests to the child that he or she *can't* behave. This is the exact opposite of what the adult wants and intends to convey! But there is an even more subtle and transparent meaning to "Can't you behave?" The question seems to imply that children, even very young children, simply *know* what behaving is and know how to do it. Much of what parents say to young children sounds like a series of variations on test questions relating back to material the child supposedly learned long before entering this world. Such questions must be very confusing for young children. Adults, however, typically hear only the conventional meaning and remain unaware of the effect their words may have. Missing is any sense of process, any recognition that *behaving* is something that has to be defined, illustrated, and cultivated by adults in order for it to develop in children. And processes take time.

As with most of these expressions, "Can't you behave!" is also a cry of exasperation. Decidedly more than just a suggestion that the child can't behave, this expression, like the rest, is part of an unending stream of negative descriptions that parents would never make if they understood how they are heard and what their impact can be, especially over time.

"Are you going to stop it?" is another question to which the knee-jerk reflex response is "No." But it is also a statement of adult impotence and powerlessness. Why would an adult who can actually control her child's behavior ask that same child if she was going to "stop it"?

"Billy, what's going on?" asked Mother matter-of-factly in response to his ear-piercing screaming in our local bookstore. Billy's mother's question came after five or six of those painfully high-pitched shrieks that only very young children can produce. While it might be nice to know what was going on in little Billy's mind, the question was empty because what this mother really wanted was for Billy not to scream.

"You're driving me crazy!" conveys to a child that the adult is at her wit's end, that she "can't take it anymore." This child must be incredibly powerful! Such exclamations constitute *negative empowerment*. Kids love power. They crave it like drugs. They'll grab up all the power adults are willing to give them. And once they begin to understand that they can push your buttons, that's exactly what they will do—over and over and over.

"It's not nice to hit Daddy" is another empty, ineffectual statement. If you're wondering what goes through the child's mind on hearing something like this, it's probably "So what!" or "It's not nice for Daddy to yell at me, either!" But what's so striking about the statement is what it's not. It is NOT an order to stop hitting Daddy. And because it's not a command, the statement is an implicit, if inadvertent, form of collusion. It says effectively "It may not be nice, but it's okay," a meaning that is conveyed and reinforced by the accompanying lack of action. Since even little children tend to be brilliant Masters of Technicalities, it is wise to assume that they will think something like "But you never told me not to hit him . . . you just said it wasn't nice."

"We're not a hitting family" and **"We don't do that"** are particularly fascinating because both statements are so obviously false. Since the child is, in fact, hitting, and since the child does, in fact, belong to the family, the family is clearly a "hitting family." This is the simple syllogistic logic at which even very young children excel.

"That's not polite" is another of those categorical statements that, for adults, carry implicit conventional meaning; in this case, "It's not polite, so don't do it." Unfortunately, adults never get around to the conventional meaning—"Don't do it!"—and then they wonder why children don't comply.

Paying attention to your everyday surroundings as if they were an unknown foreign culture can teach you important lessons very quickly. There's absolutely nothing new in the expressions that we've chosen out of the many we all hear every day. We've all heard these common expressions a million times, but most of us don't pay much attention to them. Everyday events and experiences tend to be *transparent*. In fact, most of what goes on around us is transparent in the sense that, although it's there right before our very eyes, we see right through it.

But when we look carefully, we find that the five little words in "What did I just say!?!" actually reveal more about the exasperating aspects of parenthood and child management than any other expression uttered daily by adults. Genuinely understood, this often-heard string of words contains the keys to solving a great many of the problems parents face today. What's really behind this common expression?

- A global admission of adult loss of control over often tiny children
- An implicit admission that parental words don't work
- A desperate adult demand for recognition and acknowledgment
- The implicit belief that somehow the (often public) acknowledgment of parental or adult authority will result in the desired behavior
- The implicit belief that getting another person, child or adult, to

repeat back words means that those words were understood and/or accepted

What may have at first seemed to be a complicated mess—the parent-child dynamic—becomes clearer and clearer the closer and more carefully you look and listen. This is extremely important because, although there is an immense amount of technical information out there that can be of use to parents, most of what you need to know, understand, and use is right there within your own everyday world. No advanced degree, specialty training, or traditional expert knowledge can provide what you can see, hear, and understand for yourself.

Unfortunately, if you shift your focus from the supermarket and the toy store to places where you would expect adults to be more in tune with children and more in control of what's going on—classrooms, psychiatrists' and therapists' offices, etc.—you'll see and hear the very same exchanges. The vocabulary may differ but the details of what is said and done do not. That's probably the most important reason why the increasing sophistication of professional knowledge and expertise hasn't brought about a corresponding increase in solutions to the problems of adults and children.

When it can be genuinely helpful, we'll bring in research findings from various scientific fields along the way. But such information can't replace what you can learn by paying attention to what people say and do to and with one another. It will only help us refine what we can do with our good observational skills, critical thinking, and commonsense problem-solving.

Simple and Simplistic Approaches

Because we'll offer many "simple" approaches to dealing with communication and behavior, it's important to make clear exactly what we mean by that common term. When we talk about a "simple" approach to children's behavior or learning problems or to parent-child communications, we mean that *what needs to be done can be explained and understood in straightforward commonsense terms and that the components of what needs to be done are themselves simple and can be described and understood simply.*

"Simple" does NOT mean that the process will be effortless or even short. It just means that, with patience and persistence, reasonable goals can be met without complex technology, recourse to expensive professionals or treatments. "Simplistic," on the other hand, refers to the belief, implicit in so much everyday adult behavior, that complex human problems can be solved instantaneously, with little work and often with the use of medications. Simplistic approaches relieve everyone of personal responsibility, while our simple approaches require patience and consistency and continuity over time. This doesn't mean that parenting has to be hard work. It takes no more energy to do things in a rational and problem-solving fashion than most parents are already putting into the process. It's just a different way of thinking about things, a different way of relating and communicating.

Seeing the World Differently

How hard is it to learn to see the world differently? It's not hard at all to make the necessary change in perspective—once. However, *what is more difficult is learning how to recognize and change patterns of listening, thinking, and acting.* Thinking and communication styles are *behavioral habits.* Fortunately, while it may take some effort, even ingrained habits can be changed. All that's required is a bit of self-observation, curiosity about what's happening right before our very eyes, and the willingness to put into action what we'll explain in different ways throughout this book.

Once parents begin to hear what they themselves have been saying, and once they begin to understand how children think and communicate, they can say what they really mean and mean what they really say.

2

Saying What You Mean
and Meaning What You Say

One of the easiest ways to understand the complexities of human behavior, interaction, and communication is to reduce situations to their generic components. In other words, ask simple categorical questions like "What is the parent—or what am I—really saying?" And "What is the child really hearing?"

Saying What You Mean

We were having coffee in a local café one day when a mother and her toddler sat down at the next table. Or, rather, the mother sat down and then began trying to get her child to join her. "Wouldn't you like to come sit by me?" she said, arching her eyebrows like mothers do when they're

asking a child if they'd like a treat. "How about sitting up here, next to Mommy," she continued, patting the surface of the bench right next to her. "Don't you *want* to sit with your mommy?" she said, a bit more imploringly, apparently beginning to feel as if her child didn't care about her.

Since the toddler seemed oblivious to his mother's desires, and since our new table neighbor was becoming increasingly frustrated, Denis leaned over and said with a complicitous smile, "Don't ask, *tell*." The mother smiled an understanding smile.

"Mark," the mother said gently but firmly as she patted the bench surface next to her, "come sit right here." Mark climbed up and sat down.

This little scenario just happened to take place in a coffee bar, but it's one that we have seen repeated literally hundreds of times in our office. The next time you're in a public place full of adults and children, if you watch and listen, you'll hear parents ask many questions to which there are no useful replies. There are as many classic questioning noncommands as there are opportunities to use them. Here are a few typical instances, along with a translation of the original Adultspeak.

PARENT SAYS	CHILD THINKS	PARENT MEANT	CHILD DOES
What did I just say!?!"	"You said 'Don't touch that again.'"	"Don't touch that again!"	Touches it anyway.
"How many times have I told you to knock it off!"	"Five, ten, twenty times . . . who knows!"	"Keep your feet off your brother's chair!"	Kicks his brother's chair again.
"How about leaving your sister alone for a change!"	"Well, how about it?"	"Don't interrupt your sister's reading. Leave her alone!"	Bugs his sister again.
"Don't you want to finish your squash?"	"No. I hate squash!"	"Eat the rest of your food."	Continues to stare at his plate.
"Didn't you ask me to take you to this movie?"	"Yep, I did."	"Be quiet and stop bothering all the people around us!"	Continues to talk and bug his neighbors.
"Can you say 'Thank you'?"	"Yes, I can."	"Say 'Thank you' to the nice lady."	Says nothing.

Not exactly what the parent had in mind, is it! But children, being consummate literalists, usually register *exactly* what is said.

We have found that many mothers are often very uncomfortable with issuing commands, as if, by doing so, they were being cruel and insensitive drill sergeants. "I don't like ordering my child around" we've heard so many times. But there's a very simple solution. *Any command can be phrased politely.* Just preface it with "please." We've found that once mothers (and teachers and clinicians) understand what gets communicated and what doesn't, it becomes much easier to be a benevolent authority in their children's lives. And they like the results. This is what a few of the examples, above, look like when the parent says what she means.

PARENT MEANS AND SAYS	CHILD HEARS AND THINKS	CHILD DOES
"Please don't touch that again!"	"Don't touch that again."	Doesn't touch it.
"Stop kicking your brother's chair."	"Stop kicking your brother's chair!"	Stops kicking his brother's chair.
"Stop bothering your sister!"	"Stop bothering your sister!"	Stops bothering his sister.
"Please finish everything that's on your plate."	"Finish everything that's on your plate!" Thinks, "Ugh! I hate squash!"	Says, "Squash makes me sick. Do I have to eat it, if I finish everything else?"

It's important to realize that it's not politeness in general or the addition of the word "please" that results in the child's compliance. In this case, it's the very specific fact that the parent issued a command instead of asking a question.

Do Commands Always Work?

Asking questions instead of issuing commands is just one variation on the massive theme of parent-child miscommunication, but parents could save themselves an immense amount of grief if they paid attention to this one detail and changed their communication styles accordingly.

Still, it's important to realize that no approach to communication can *guarantee* that your child will always hear exactly what you mean and always follow your directions.

If children do refuse to comply or if they tune you out, it won't be because you gave them the opportunity to do so by using a confused communication style. And it will leave the door open for reasonable noncompliant responses, such as when the child protested that he didn't like squash. You are then free to choose whether to stick with what you've just said or to be flexible and give the child a range of options such as "Okay, you don't have to eat your squash. Just finish the rest of what you have." This way, you are much more likely to get what you want—understanding and reasonable compliance—while your child will be more able to please you without having to sacrifice his individuality in the process.

Meaning What You Say

We've already pointed out that parents assume that they can rely on *conventional meaning* to carry their message. But conventional meaning backfires as often as it prevails.

Moe is the school bully who picks on Calvin because he's a smart aleck who still carries his stuffed tiger around. Here, however, Calvin is really more like a parent who thinks he's making a point—namely, that Moe's bullying days are limited—and who assumes that Moe will get his message as intended and stop his bullying sooner rather than later. Calvin counted on Moe hearing what he meant, not acting on what he actually said. But, instead, Moe reacts just like a kid. He does exactly what Calvin tells him to do.

All too often, parents say exactly the opposite of what they mean:

CALVIN AND HOBBES © 1992 Watterson. Reprinted with permission of UNIVERSAL PRESS SYNDICATE. All rights reserved.

- "Just say that again!"
- "Go ahead. Touch that toy and see what happens!"
- "Hit your sister and see what happens to you!"
- "Okay, don't clean up your room and see what your dad does when he gets home."

We all have a tendency to believe that the more intensely we mean something, the clearer and more intense our message is. Yet look at what was actually said in the common expressions above. Each is a command to do exactly the opposite of what the parent wanted and intended. The fourth example above could have been said in a calm matter-of-fact tone. But, for the most part, contradictory commands tend to pop out during moments of anger and intense frustration, often at a time when a parent feels defeated and powerless. This means that both parent and child are in the grips of un-thought-out reflex reactions, and this radically increases the likelihood that the child will respond to the literal content rather than the parent's intended meaning.

Emotion as Communication

Emotions are behavioral states that another person can recognize—delight, surprise, fear, anxiety, anger, sadness, and empathy. Every attentive mother and father has watched the two universal emotional indicators, smiling and crying, give rise to more distinct and differentiated emotion signals as the infant grows in its relationship with its caregivers. Empathy is an emotion that tends to enhance communication—or at least it enhances the experience of connectedness and feeling understood. The one emotion that most contaminates parent-child communication, and that so often derails it, is anger.

When you discipline with anger—or, worse yet, rage—your emotion becomes the central focus of the child's experience. For all intents and purposes, the negative emotion *is* the communication. When that change of focus occurs, *you* have become the focus of the child's experience, not whatever behavior you're trying to change. This allows the child to change the subject entirely and protest, "You're being mean to me!" Once that shift occurs, you're likely to end up in a tug-of-war over who's being mean to whom. The original issue will have been lost.

It's safe to assume that the child will forget whatever he was just doing as intense negative emotion triggers his own emotions. *Emotion can drive content right out of conscious awareness.* At this point you're likely to get denials, which can lead to the feeling that that the child is lying, which, in turn, provokes further denials—all of which fuels a self-perpetuating vicious cycle of mutual anger.

When a child runs into the street, all we want is for the child to stop and look and not get hit by a car. But it's difficult to react in a calm, unemotional way when we see our offspring with traffic bearing down. We scream, but the intense parental emotion may simply cause the child to freeze. Or he may turn to respond to the familiar angry tone when he hears his name called, causing him to be hit by the car. We want emotion to increase the effectiveness of verbal communication, not take its place.

The dangers of emotional reactions seem pretty obvious, so why do parents so often react this way? One reason dates way back to our own childhood. Unless we had ice-cold indifferent parents as young children, we all experienced an increase in success in getting what we wanted when we cried. Even if our parents were wise enough not to be manipulated by temper tantrums, only the most insensitive of parents would not respond to genuine sadness and give in often enough to create an experiential pattern that linked expressions of sadness and disappointment with getting what we wanted. Crying and anger become confused early in development. Very young children cry out of frustration and anger and not just sadness and loss. All in all, we tend to grow into life with a primitive sense that anger "works."

But unless you want to teach your child that anger and other intense negative emotions *are* the essence of communication, use such emotions sparingly. And, if after an extended period of not reacting and communicating angrily, you unexpectedly do explode and your child complies with lightning speed, don't conclude that anger worked. The momentary "success" will have been due to surprise and novelty, not to the communication effectiveness of anger.

Don't Count on Authority or Tradition to Say What You Mean

Many parents use nursery rhymes, fairy tales, or religious stories both to entertain their children and to communicate values. However, just as expressions have both conventional and literal meanings, so too can such cherished rhymes, poems, stories, and prayers. Adults tend to confuse *conventional experience* and communication. After all, the context in which we heard these things recited was usually a very warm, supportive, and positive one. The experience of hearing these rhymes and stories read to us was good. So what we remember fondly is the experience, not the literal content.

All you have to do to see how well-intentioned adults inadvertently create problems for themselves and their children is to listen carefully to what is actually being said. Remember this common prayer?

> *Now I lay me down to sleep.*
> *I pray the Lord my soul to keep.*
> *If I should die before I wake,*
> *I pray the Lord my soul to take.*

What caring parent would want to suggest to her three- or four-year-old that she could *die* during the night! While struggling to protect their children by restricting their access to television or other sources of news about the horrors of life on this planet, parents often remain unaware of the disturbing literal meaning of the words they repeat routinely night after night. Yet there they are, routinely suggesting to their own children that they may not survive the next ten hours.

Or how about this nursery rhyme, which is recited to infants and very young children, even sung soothingly as mothers rock their children to sleep:

> *Rock-a-bye, baby, in the treetop,*
> *When the wind blows, the cradle will rock;*
> *When the bough breaks, the cradle will fall,*
> *Down will come baby, cradle and all.*

Contrast this with a nursery rhyme that has been around for a lot longer yet:

> *Ring around the rosie.*
> *Pocket full of posie.*
> *Ashes, ashes.*
> *All fall down.*

While these familiar words may conjure up visions of happy little children dancing around a Maypole, this beloved nursery rhyme is really about the Black Plague! The "ring around the rosie" refers to the ringed rosaceous spots that appear on the skin of the dying plague victim. "Posie" refers to the crushed dried flowers that medieval physicians threw into the air in the sick person's room, hoping to drive out the bad humors that were thought to cause such afflictions. "Ashes, ashes" is a corruption of "Achoo! Achoo!"—the uncontrollable sneezing that comes on as bubonic plague becomes pneumonic plague. And, finally, "All fall down" means "All fall down dead."

Today, when a mother or father says to a child "Let me kiss your boo-boo and make it better," the parent is actually using a term whose lineage can be traced directly back to the buboes of the black plague.

Empty Meaning

But what children hear in rhymes like "Ring Around the Rosie" are the rhyming words and the rhythm, not the original meaning. One might say that the present, contemporary meaning is "empty." The words may as well be ciphers or nonsense syllables like Lewis Carroll's "Jabberwocky." A meaning key is needed to decipher them. The passage of time and scientific, medical, and technological progress, as well as the force of convention, drive the original meaning out of much traditional language and lore. These relics of childhood are fun precisely because they still belong to a magic time, not because of what they say.

Active Meaning

Unlike "Ring Around the Rosie," nursery rhymes like "Rock-a-bye, Baby" and prayers like "Now I Lay Me Down to Sleep" are full of *active meaning*. No special knowledge is required to understand the meaning of "Down will come baby, cradle and all!" No historical keys are required to decipher "If I should die before I wake . . ." The meaning is right there. It just tends to be transparent and invisible because we react to the spirit of the tradition, not to the strikingly obvious content. Certainly, parents who recite or sing such nursery rhymes to their children, or who share such bedtime prayers with them, do not intend to instill terror. Nor do they intend to undermine their children's trust in benevolent parental protection. And they certainly don't want to scare them into staying awake all night. And yet that's often the result of such good intentions.

The Bible Is an Exception, Right?

Whenever anything becomes an Ultimate Authority, people tend to abandon simple common sense. For many people, the Bible is one such Ultimate Authority, the source of everything true and a reference guide to the meaning of life. Yet because children, especially very young children, tend to hear exactly what the words say, they may come away from reading the Bible or hearing Bible stories with an understanding that is very different from what was intended by their elders. And children may apply biblical lessons in a manner that is also very different from what was intended.

One mother, who was very involved in various church and Christian parents' and children's groups, was quite surprised when her four-year-old said to her, "You told me, Mommy, not to do revenge and not to hit my brother back when he hits me. But God does revenge. And it says so in the Bible!"

"What do you mean?" she said, stunned.

"Well, like when He made the big flood. He was mad. He killed all the bad people except Noah. And that's revenge. So, if I'm mad, I can too do revenge! Because God did it! And it's in the Bible. I know. I learned it in Sunday School." Not knowing what to reply to her four-year-old, the mother just changed the subject. A few minutes later, her four-year-old came back. "And you know what?" he said. "I don't think the Ark was really real."

"Why?" she asked, a little overwhelmed by her four-year-old's stream of Bible commentary.

"Because you couldn't get all those animals on just one boat!" he stated matter-of-factly. "You just couldn't. Because one boat's too small."

With this he shook his head as if it were obvious and anyone ought to see it. When she told us this story, the mother described herself as very lucky that her son took such a matter-of-fact approach to his comments on the Bible. "What would I have done if he had demanded that I explain all those things," she said with a look of amazement. "And he's only four!"

If you choose to use the Bible or other sacred writings as the model for personal values, it's wise to assume that even very young children will note contradictions and inconsistencies, because they will. And even young children will demand explanations. If you don't make clear the inconsistencies and provide an alternate justification for the values you want to communicate, your children may feel that it is entirely appropriate to use such an unassailable authority as the justification for behavior they otherwise clearly know is wrong.

3

Childhood Thinking and the Logic of Language

The Myth of Childhood Illogic

With the exception of a very few pockets of realistic child development research, the prevailing view in the overall child studies world is that children have a long developmental path to tread on the way to logical thinking. According to the reigning model in American education and mental health, children are "prelogical" and do not become logical thinkers until the developmentally "geriatric" age of eleven to fifteen years. This is a very curious belief since so much of everyday experience demonstrates the very opposite—that children are, in fact, logical thinkers from the very beginning.

Lessons from the Comic Strips

The most consistent theme in the nonpolitical comic strips is the language and logic of childhood thinking. Over the years, some cartoonists have captured these brilliantly. Everyone laughs at cartoons like these. How true, cartoon-reading parents say, that's just what children think!

DENNIS THE MENACE

"I GIVE UP. HOW MANY TIMES **DO** YOU HAVE TO TELL ME TO BEHAVE?"

DENNIS THE MENACE used by permission of Hank Ketcham and © by North America Syndicate.

And there are many such cartoons week after week, month after month, year after year. This is the other side of the "What did I just say!?!" coin. Dennis the Menace has been put in the corner, doubtless, as so many parents say, "to think about his behavior." And, yes, "I give up. How many times *do* you have to tell me to behave?" does sound flippant and disrespectful. *But it is the absolutely perfectly logical response to Dennis's mother's question.* This isn't illogic at work. This is the very essence of logic. And Dennis, like your five-year-old or the eight-year-old next door, doesn't have to wait until his eleventh to fifteenth birthday to start to think logically.

Like Hank Ketcham, Bill Watterson also understands the link between words and thought in children's thinking and experience.

When Calvin says "I obey the letter of the law," he's talking about logic, semantics, and the literal meaning of words. Calvin is Everychild's Technicality Meister par excellence, full of linguistic *Gotcha!*s. Calvin's mom wants him "in the tub," so that's exactly what Calvin gives her: he gets "in the tub." The story could have gone on and on with Calvin stretching the whole thing out as long as he could. "Good first step!" Mom might have said. "Now I want to hear that water running!" So

CALVIN AND HOBBES © 1990 Watterson. Reprinted with permission of Universal Press Syndicate. All rights reserved.

Calvin would have turned on the faucet so his mother could have heard the water running—which was, of course, exactly what she had asked for. Eventually Calvin might have to fill up the tub with water, take off his clothes, and actually get in and take a bath. But not until he had exhausted every conceivable linguistic technicality!

Masters or Victims of Logic?

Only part of the time are any of us in charge of our understanding and use of language. Children are just a special case, locked as they are into literal meaning and logic even more than adults.

Remember Abbott and Costello's famous "Who's on first?" routine? Or the scene from another movie where they find a magic lantern while rummaging around in a pile of junk? When Lou Costello picks up the lantern and begins to polish it with his coat sleeve, a huge genie appears and says, "Your wish is my command." Since Costello is always thinking about food, he instantly replies, "Make me a malted!" And the genie turns him into a gigantic malted milkshake. That's the logic of language. Costello was absolutely conscious in saying what he said, he just didn't mean it the way the genie heard it.

One mother told us a story about her four-year-old daughter, who came running into the kitchen saying, "It's the ice cream man. Can I have some money for an ice cream bar?" Her mother had heard the bell, too, but recognized it as the warning bell that sounds when certain vehicles back up. When her daughter wouldn't accept her categorical explanation that it was the wrong day for the ice cream truck to be in the neighborhood, the mom went to the window to see what had made the noise.

"That's not the ice cream man," the mom said. "It's the plumber. He's backing his truck up."

"Okay," her daughter replied, "then I'll have a plum!"

Most of the time, as conscious as children may be of using the words they use, *they have no idea that their meanings are different than our meanings*. When the three-year-old exclaims that "germs come from Germany," he's not trying to be the next Robin Williams. He may laugh when we laugh, but he means what he says, and it is entirely logical.

Years ago we worked with a very bright five-year-old who had hor-rible night fears and was terrified of being put to bed by her father. On the basis of the information the parents provided on the intake sheet, we were pretty certain we knew what was going on. All we had to do was to ask this father, in the presence of his daughter, what he did for a living.

"I work at the county animal shelter," the dad replied. He then had one of those *Egads! I just realized what I've been doing all this time!* looks and shook his head yes as he said very slowly, "And I put animals to sleep . . ."

Adults are constantly trying to soften the blow of experience—or sim-ply trying not to face reality as it is—by creating euphemisms. Instead of dying, Grandpa "passed" or "expired." ("You mean we subscribed to him?!?" said one young child.) Although it sounds brutal, when we asked the dad if he really "put dogs to sleep" or whether he actually *killed* them, he explained that his job was to give the animals a shot that killed them. Because even many young children have heard expressions such as "rest in peace" or "sleeping with the angels," we also explained carefully that neither dead animals nor dead people sleep. Death is death and sleep is sleep.

To make sure that his daughter understood the distinction between people and animals, we asked if people were ever given shots to kill them. Even though both he and we knew that euthanasia was both legal and practiced in some parts of the world and that some American states use lethal injection to execute prisoners who are condemned to death, the dad replied with a categorical "NO," and that was that. His daughter's nighttime anxiety disappeared as of our meeting, as did her fear of having her father put her to bed. (We're not avoiding the issue of categorical

DENNIS THE MENACE

"MR. WILSON SAYS I'M A NOYING. WHAT'S A NOYING?"

DENNIS THE MENACE used by permission of Hank Ketcham and © by North America Syndicate.

"truth" here. We'll deal with issues of truth, honesty, and the need to know in chapter 9.)

This five-year-old with nighttime fears—who, incidentally, also tried to keep a bridal shower from ending because the bride hadn't "taken her shower yet"— illustrates the *obligatory* aspect of childhood logic. Words mean what they mean. And that's often what they continue to mean until they're given new and different meanings. Whether it's "taking a shower" or "putting to sleep" or "germs from Germany," words and phrases have only those meanings that the child has thus far learned. And until they're spelled out, words are also nothing but sounds. So if bakers sell baked goods, then plum(b)ers sell plums.

Children are brilliant observers. One of the reasons they learn language so effectively and efficiently is that they recognize important patterns amidst the inconsistent jumble of their speech environment. One of the patterns they recognize on their own is that definite and indefinite articles like *the* or *a(n)* indicate that a noun follows immediately, as in *the house* or *a tree*. So Dennis, who obviously hasn't learned the word *annoying* yet, treats the sounds that compose it as two words. After all, it's a perfectly logical application of one of the rules of grammar. It takes a long time for children to begin to understand the incredible subtleties of meaning, meaning that can change profoundly depending upon context and what the speaker intends to convey.

In the following illustration, Marilyn, Saddam Hussein, and the Pasta Roni box are all saying exactly the same thing, yet the meaning of those two words is very different in each case. In the first instance, we're dealing with a movie star whose seductiveness made her a cultural icon. In

the second, we're dealing with a defiant dictator who behaves much like a consciousless kid with unlimited power: first he says "Make me!" then he gives in, only to say "Make me!" again. As for the ready-to-fix food people, they just want you to buy and consume their product. It's important not to lose sight of the fact that what makes us chuckle as we look at these three versions of the same two-word expression is an adult understanding of content and intent that has been provided by decades of experience that children, especially very young children, have yet to gain.

Logic acts on meaning, and the results are meaningful. Logic always "makes sense," even if it's not *about* anything at all. Because children's minds have to be adept at manipulating symbols logically, they are brilliant calculators from the beginning of life. Children can do these operations with lightning speed. Their manipulations lead to logical conclusions—and part of our human nature is to be satisfied by meaningfulness and logical conclusions. So children's logical manipulations often lead them down the path of meaning but away from the way things really are.

Logic and Children's Understanding

Where Do Babies Come From?

What's one of the most common answers that parents give to this question? We heard it so often from both parents and children we were working with that we decided to do a little experiment. We asked a friend who taught a fourth-grade class of nine- and ten-year-olds to give her class the in-class project of writing a very short essay entitled "Before I Was Born." The children were asked to describe where they were before they were born and what was going on at the time. Here's a typical essay:

> My mom got a prescription from the doctor. So she got the medi-cine. And took one and her stomach grew fat. When the pill grew, I came out. I saw all the blood and at dinner food fell on my head. And I had to take a blood bath. And the blood took me to the heart. And I saw a germ. I went back to the stomach. And then I went to the intestines and then I came out. Plop! plop! plop! plop! [spelling corrected]

Yikes! This nine-year-old fourth grader thinks that he was pooped into the world! But isn't this perfectly logical if he was in his mother's *stomach* before he was born? How else would the baby get out? If you think that we're exaggerating, consider that nineteen out of the twenty-three children in this fourth-grade class placed themselves in their mother's stomach prior to being born.

Making Babies

Once, when the subject of childhood logic came up, a dad we were working with started to laugh and said, "I've got to tell you a story." He said that he and his four-year-old were out playing in a park when his son noticed two dogs copulating. A bit embarrassed and caught off guard when his son wanted to know what the two dogs were doing, the dad replied, "They're making a puppy," and led his son off in a different direction. Not long after the park incident, the four-year-old wandered into his parents' bedroom in the middle of the night. He looked stunned at his father, who was on top of his mother.

"Daddy, what are you doing to Mommy?" the boy asked.

"We're making a baby," the dad blurted out, again caught off guard.

"Can't you turn Mommy over?" the four-year-old asked. "I'd rather have a puppy!"

The Attack of the Bad Ducks

To help our child therapy colleagues understand the logic of children's thinking we included another anecdote in our earlier book, *Healing the Hurt Child*. Danny, a four-year-old boy who we were helping with his anger problems, also had a morbid fear of "bad ducks." He thought they were lurking about the house, under his bed, and even in the ceiling. But mostly he thought that they were up over his bed. This turned bedtime into a nightly struggle full of fears, tears, and unending parental reassurances that there were no bad ducks "up there" or anywhere else in Danny's room.

We discovered the origins of this four-year-old's fear of ducks quite serendipitously nearly a year later. The boy's father was explaining how he and a friend had dealt with the aftermath of Hurricane Elena. The storm had damaged each of their homes in a different way that just happened to correspond to the other friend's area of job expertise. Danny's dad worked in general construction, while the friend was an air-conditioning specialist. Danny was playing in his room when the friend came through, accompanied by Danny's parents.

"What's wrong?" Danny asked, picking up on everyone's obvious worry.

"Bad ducts," the air-conditioning specialist replied. "Lots of them."

"Where?" Danny wanted to know.

"All over," said the friend, "but mostly up there, over your bed."

Many people make little distinction between words that end in a *ct* sound and those without the final *t* as in expressions such as "keeping track" or "keeping tract." Danny's "bad ducks" were nothing more than "bad ducts." We all laughed when we realized the origin of his intense fears. But the fact that Danny had "simply misunderstood a word" didn't make the fears we were then able to dispel any less real.

4

Children Live in a Very Different World

"Whatcha doin'?" Sam asks.

"I'm going to put some fertilizer on the lawn," Dad replies.

"Why?"

"Because the grass needs its food, just like you, Sam."

"Why?"

"Because without its food, the grass will turn brown. And maybe die." Sam's father pours the dry fertilizer into the spreader, being careful to stop right at the "full" line. "Gotta stop right there," he says.

"What if you put too much?"

"If you put too much fertilizer on, it can burn the grass."

"And it'll catch on fire?"

"No." Sam's dad smiles. "It'll just turn it brown. Or, if you put too much on, it'll kill the grass. But that's what the hose is for. I water it in after I put the fertilizer on."

"What if you use too much water?"

"Then you'd wash it all away."

"What if there's no water?" Sam adds, remembering that his family had gone without water for two days in their old neighborhood when the city renovated a water main.

"Then we'd have to be careful not to put too much on."

This exchange between Sam and his dad is not just informational. True, Sam doesn't know the factual answers to his questions, so they do have an informational aspect to them. But there's more here than meets the eye. Adults look down on children from their perspective of decades of experience, experience that has defined and refined everything they know, and forget that children don't share that perspective. So what Sam is really saying is "Why are things the way they are? Daddy, please tell me that I can count on this world to be reliable, to hold together. Please reassure me that everything's going to be okay. *Because I don't know.*"

"Why is there something and not nothing?" a six-year-old asked his father. Later that night, the man was stunned to find his son's question as the first sentence in the opening chapter of Martin Heidegger's *An Introduction to Metaphysics*. Some adults, who tend to be philosophers and other intellectuals, are plagued by questions born of uncertainty and the incompleteness of knowledge. But these questions are the fundamental questions of childhood. Many four- or five-year-olds are asking them daily, though few adults really hear them or take them seriously. Adults quickly forget that what the world is, why it holds together, and why it is more or less the same from day to day is not self-evident. The relative sameness of the world is *familiar*. We all grow into it. It's easy to take it for granted. But every now and then that familiarity breaks down and *why the world is as it is* becomes a puzzle that can be curious, troubling, or even terrifying.

Why? What If . . . ? How Come?

Sam's questions make for a good introduction to the world of childhood experience and how it differs from the world of adult experience. All young children ask these questions. In fact, it's because they're so common and because they tend to peak at a particular moment in childhood, roughly between the ages of four to six, that parents often refer to this time in their child's life as "the 'What if . . .' stage."

Some children just ask these questions every now and then and little seems to depend upon the replies they get. Other children, most often boys, pour out "What if?" questions in an unending stream that can exhaust parents, who wonder why their children never seem satisfied with the answers they get. By looking at what parents actually say to children in response to these questions, we can learn a lot about both childhood experience and parent-child communication.

Why Is the Grass Green?

When young children ask questions like "Why is the grass green?" *a very few* actually may be asking for complex technical answers to their questions. Most, however, want to know why the grass is green and not blue or red or some other color. Since, for very young children, there really are no answers to such questions, it makes more sense to treat them simply as requests for reassurance that things are the way they are simply because they're supposed to be that way. If you rush to an encyclopedia-style answer and begin talking about chlorophyll and photosynthesis, you'll just fill your child's head with empty words and phrases, but you won't satisfy your child's basic need for certainty and reassurance. In this case, you will actually be increasing your child's need to know that there's a reason why the world is the way it is—and the questions will only multiply.

If, on the other hand, you say something categorical like "Well, because that's the way it is" or, if you're more inclined to such explanations, "Because God made the grass green," you will probably satisfy your child's immediate need for a simple reassuring answer. Such answers are not dismissive. They're simply reassuring categorical responses to questions about the categorical structure of the world. If you take this approach with very young children, you'll find that the repetitive questions ease up. When they do, you can conclude that the questions were driven by a need for certainty, not by a need for detailed information.

Where Did I Come From?—Again

Many parents—and many child experts—think that children's questions should be answered according to their ability to understand. Answer such questions, they suggest, according to where the child is developmentally. But we think this is the wrong approach. The issue is not what the child is capable of understanding but, instead, *what the child is asking.*

When a three-year-old says, "Where did I come from?" many parents go into a premature panic because they assume that this question means the same thing to their child that it does to them. Usually this conjures up the "s" word—SEX. But it can have other complicated meanings as well. With adopted children, for example, it can mean the whole complex adoption situation. Over nearly two decades, we've met hundreds of parents who answered these very simple childhood questions with long explanations about human reproduction or contorted apologetic explanations of why women give away babies. But that's not what very young children are asking. That's what adults are thinking and worried about.

Children aren't asking for adult explanations for sensitive or embarrassing adult issues. Their questions reflect a much narrower context of highly personal meaning defined by their limited experience and the often tight, categorical meaning of words. Many adult answers often presuppose a wealth of experience and learning that children simply do not have.

Even Calvin, who is decidedly more than a toddler, is only asking a generic, basic, fundamental question. As complex, devious, creative, detail-minded, and intelligent as Calvin may be, he's still carrying around his stuffed tiger. He's still a little kid. He's not asking for—*and he doesn't*

need—complex real-world technical answers to his basic, fundamental questions. Bill Watterson may have upped the ante by making the kitchen the context for Calvin's question. Remember, everyday language places babies in Mother's stomach. But he also knows that the "making babies" context resonates more with his readers' preoccupations than with Calvin's. This allows Calvin's dad to play his sadistic game with his son by switching back to the real childhood issue of where babies come from. Calvin's experience is still so limited that the "real" answers to his questions would only kill the magic of his fantasy-filled childhood and make him ashamed to be palling around with a stuffed tiger.

But Won't My Child Accuse Me Later of Lying?

This is another adult worry that doesn't take into account the realities of childhood experience. Questions like "Where did I come from?" and "Why is the grass green?" are as much about parent-child relationships as they are about birth and the color of grass. The kind of generic answers that we recommend are reassuring for the young child. They reinforce the idea that things are the way they are for a reason and that there's no need to worry. A child who grows up in a basically comfortable relationship with a parent won't think bad things about that parent. In fact, all of these things blend so imperceptibly into the flow of everyday experience that children who can basically count on their parents won't even remember these issues in true-or-false terms.

Later, when your child is seven or eight and comes to you saying, "Don't give me the 'God made it that way' answer. Come on now, why *is* the grass green?" then, of course, it does make sense to begin to give those complex explanations that only confuse little minds and create empty vocabularies that mislead adults into thinking their child knows what he's talking about. It's easy to tell when a child is asking you a series of truly informational questions because she will ask for clarifications. Children have an insatiable hunger for knowledge and are constantly wondering and inquiring. If the questions are about a task or something that can be explored by looking and touching, she may continue the process by seeing for herself. It's not hard to see when a child is pursuing a particular idea or refining details out of curiosity and a hunger for details.

Parents Usually Say Much
More Than They Think They Do

Because even little children often use the same words we do, we all have a tendency to assume that these words have the same meaning in terms of vocabulary *and* experience. So adults use words very loosely. But we already know that because children, especially very young children, are logical thinkers, they tend to think and reason in very narrow and literal fashion. This means that they often hear something very different than what we think we're saying.

The "Burning" Questions of Childhood

Let's return to Sam and his father to see what else may have been going on in Sam's mind. Sam's father answered his son's questions in a simple matter-of-fact manner, assuming without even being aware of doing so that the words he used meant the same thing to Sam that they did to him. But the words parents use to communicate with their children are full of multiple meanings, meanings that may be innocuous in one context and literally terrifying in another. This doesn't typically present a problem for adults because they've had decades of practice in switching from one context to another, so typically adults don't think twice when they use words like "burn" and "kill" and "die," words that, when applied to grass, aren't terribly worrisome but when applied to people can be very scary.

When Sam asked his dad why he was going to put that strange powder on the grass, his dad replied, "Because the grass needs its food, just like you, Sam." So fertilizer is just like food. In fact, we routinely talk about "plant food" and "lawn food" without giving these terms a second thought. Sam's dad extended the comparison by telling his son that the grass needs food to live, perhaps much as he or Sam's mother had replied to another question at another time by saying that people eat food because our bodies need it to stay alive. But Sam's dad didn't stop there. He went on to add that without the "food," the grass could turn brown "and maybe die." This may be the first time that Sam actually thought that he could die if he didn't eat.

But no sooner does Sam's dad inform him about the vital function of food than he throws his son a subtle but powerful meaning curve. He adds that the fertilizer—the "grass food"—can "burn" the grass. We can see that Sam is thinking both literally and logically when he asks if the grass will catch fire. Sam's dad smiles because he sees the humor. And he straightens out his son's thinking by saying that the grass won't really catch on fire, it will only turn brown. But Sam's dad fails to appreciate the significance of his son's pristine logic and doesn't realize that he has introduced the notion that *food can kill*. Perhaps at this moment Sam will remember the rat poison on the top shelf in the garage that his dad puts out for rats to *eat* . . . .

We've seen many otherwise absolutely normal children over the years who had developed this or that food fear because of the logical conclusions that they had drawn from casual remarks made by their parents.

Why Adults Don't Hear What They're Actually Saying

The stock market doesn't really go *up* and we don't really *kill* government programs or legislation. We don't really *have* time, *waste* time, or *run out* of time. And nothing really *costs* us time. We don't really *fire* people or *can* them. And we certainly don't *give them a lift*. We don't *handle people with kid gloves* or *tread softly* with others. Children don't really *get on our nerves* or *drive us crazy*. We don't really sleep *like a log*. And we're never *dead tired*.

Because we literally grow into such metaphorical expressions as we grow into language and life, by the time we're even old enough to think seriously about these things, we're already so steeped in metaphor that most of us never become aware of it.

Now, if it's that hard for mature adults to become consciously aware of metaphor, imagine what a big challenge it represents for little logical thinkers!

Take Advantage of These Moments

Some children are unusually sensitive to the logic of language and may be very troubled by literal meanings or logical connections that aren't immediately obvious. These children sometimes look mesmerized, often staring directly at you while asking their questions or perhaps staring into space. Often, but not always, you can tell that they are actually visualizing the consequences of the logical links—like the grass catching on fire—because their eyes move as if focused on a movement-filled scenario even when they're looking right at you. When this happens, it is best to drop whatever activity you're involved in and take a few moments to explore your child's thinking right then and there.

By pursuing the issue when your child is deeply engrossed in intense meanings and logical connections, you can help prevent anxiety-provoking misunderstandings. Not only can these moments allow you to undo confusions and straighten out misunderstandings, they can also strengthen your relationship with your child as you help make the world more understandable and less scary.

You don't have to purge your vocabulary of words like "fire," "burn," and "die." It's not necessary and, besides, it's impossible: language is a constant stream of metaphors and images. And many children simply go with the flow of everyday language just like adults. If you do detect a tone of worry or anxiousness as your child drags out a series of "Why/What if?" questions in an attempt to come to a reassuring conclusion, just explain the conventional meaning of the words. "We call fertilizer 'food' because plants need what's in it to grow. But the good food we eat can't kill us." In our practice, when parents use expressions like "dead tired" or "dead asleep," we interrupt and say to the parent, "People aren't really dead when they're sleeping, are they?" After the parent laughs and says no, we explain, even to three-and-a-half and four-year-olds, "That's just an expression—like 'raining cats and dogs.'" Many young children will then add other "funny" expressions.

Sometimes the only indication that a child has been troubled by what they've heard is the appearance of separation anxiety or sleep disturbance. Just think back over the events and discussions of the last few days and ask yourself how those things might look or sound from a young child's point of view. And, of course, ask the child what they're worrying about. (Remember to "ask" with a command: "Tell me what's worrying you" not "Are you worried about anything?")

At other times, however, these apparently endless streams of questions are simply *contact extenders*, a way of keeping the adult engaged in the exchange. When this is the case, you can usually break the connection without breaking the relationship by redirecting the child into another activity. If the child is relationship-hungry because he or she genuinely hasn't had enough of you, you may find it much harder to disengage from these series of empty questions. The cure for this is to be more tuned-in to your child on an everyday basis and to engage in more meaningful activities together. You'll find specific ways to do this in the next chapter and in chapter 13.

Children also love the sense of being in control, of being in charge of what's going on. Some children may play out a string of *"Why?"* *"What if?"* and *"How come?"* questions just to exercise this power. It's not too hard to tell when this is happening because, at some point in the process, the child, usually eight or older, can no longer conceal her delight in stringing you on. When this happens, don't get angry or feel manipulated. Just say something like "Boy, did you have me going!" This gives the child (or early adolescent) credit for her moment of mastery without turning it into a power struggle. And then move on to whatever is appropriate at the time. Do NOT treat such language and relationship play as a challenge to your authority. If you do, you will inadvertently teach the child how to get your goat and be in charge of your behavior.

The World Is as the World Seems

Many years ago we received a frantic call from an irate mother who could not manage to calm her child. Her two-and-a-half-year-old had had an intensely negative reaction to an antihistamine prescribed by a doctor at a local walk-in clinic. The antihistamine caused an acute hallucinatory crisis in which the two-and-a-half-year-old saw the butterflies on his bedspread and curtains coming after him. At first, not even closing his eyes would get rid of them. By the time the mother called us, two days had passed and the "bad butterflies" had not gone away. The mother was so frustrated and so angry that she was ready to sue the doctor and the clinic. She could barely get her child back into the house because of his terror, let alone get him to enter his bedroom or sleep in his own bed.

On the phone, Debbie told the mother to buy a plastic spray bottle at the local hardware store and to fill it half full of water and then add just a touch of perfume. She told the mother to put the butterfly bedspread back on her son's bed and to put the curtains back up in her son's bedroom. The mom was then instructed to tell her two-and-a-half-year-old that she had bought a "magic spray that turns bad butterflies into good butterflies." With her son present, the mother was then to make a big production out of carefully spraying the door frame to her child's bedroom as well as the curtains and the bedspread and then to treat the bedroom as perfectly normal and safe. Her son's anxiety decreased over the course of the day, the "bad butterflies" disappeared, and he slept comfortably in his own bed that night.

It's hard enough for adults to regain their sense of safety and security after toxic hallucinatory experiences, which feel very real at any age. Yet the adult can use the perspective of a lifetime to compare, judge, and determine whether the content of an experience was *really* real. For children, especially very young children, such chemically induced experiences simply *are* real. Children simply don't have the rich psychological archive that allows their elders to put things in perspective. So words are a waste of time.

Of course, you talk to young children in distress, but put the message you want your child to receive into what you do. Remember that Debbie didn't give this two-and-a-half-year-old's mother a prescription for reassuring words. The only words Debbie told the mother to use were those that described the effects of the "magic spray that turns bad butterflies into good butterflies." Without the magic spray, the mother's words would have been empty. (We had given out hundreds of samples of "Ghost-Away!" long before anyone had thought up Ghostbusters!) The hallucinations brought on by this toddler's atypical response to the antihistamine turned his safe and reliable world upside down. For very young children, the only real antidote to one kind of experience is another kind of experience.

5

Logic, Experience, and
Childhood Fears

What every parent needs to know about children, their thinking, and
their experience is actually the foundation for what every expert needs to
know—not vice versa. Nowhere can this be seen more clearly than in
some of the myths about children's developmental abilities that are still
at the heart of what students and professionals are taught in education,
psychology, and psychiatry. Because the reigning developmental model in
these fields defines categorically what children supposedly can and cannot do at any given "stage," students, teachers, researchers, and clinicians
are typically quite satisfied with the spontaneous responses that children
give to developmental task questions. But what children say and what
they actually think and believe are not necessarily the same.

One of the most famous developmental task questions has to do with
how children think about the inanimate (nonliving) world. If you consult the standard texts in child psychiatry, for example, you'll learn that
children are animists, meaning that children really do think that things
like rocks and the moon are alive. Or, as Bruno Bettelheim put it in *The
Uses of Enchantment*, his extremely popular book on the psychoanalytic
meaning of fairy tales:

> To the eight-year-old (to quote Piaget's examples), the sun is alive
> because it gives light (and, one may add, it does that because it

wants to). To the child's animistic mind, the stone is alive because it can move, as it rolls down a hill. Even a twelve-and-a-half-year-old is convinced that a stream is still alive and has a will, because its water is flowing. The sun, the stone, and the water are believed to be inhabited by spirits very much like people, so they feel and act like people.

We want parents to be infinitely more curious about real children than either Bruno Bettelheim or Jean Piaget, whose developmental stage psychology still defines what the American education and psychiatry establishments think they know about children. Bettelheim and Piaget spent much more time describing children than they did actually talking with them. And in all those famous studies conducted by Piaget and his very famous students and collaborators at his Center for Genetic Epistemology at the University of Geneva, *no child was ever interviewed more than once.* Why? Because it was never necessary. Children typically give the "right" answer very quickly or they give the right "wrong" answer just as fast. Either way, the process is quickly over.

Here's a classic Piagetian interview that appears to demonstrate with a real four- or five-year-old just what Bettelheim claimed above:

> INTERVIEWER: Is the moon alive?
> CHILD: Um-hmm, it is.
> INTERVIEWER: How do you know?
> CHILD: Because it follows me when I walk.
> INTERVIEWER: How do you know it follows you?
> CHILD: Because when I move, it moves.

As soon as the child gives the answer predicted by Piagetian stage psychology, the interview comes to an end. The interviewer is content to have demonstrated once again that children think exactly as described by eight decades of Piagetian research.

This is very much like the exchange between Sam and his father. Sam's dad accepted that he and his son were talking about exactly the same things in exactly the same way. According to common assumptions, not only were their words the same, so were the meanings of the words and the experiences to which the words corresponded. Had Sam's dad been struck by his son's very logical conclusion that the grass could catch on fire because fertilizer "can burn the grass," he might have discovered that his son's inner world was immensely richer—and, at times, much more scary—than he had ever imagined. The same is true for well over half a decade of child psychology and psychiatry in this country. Researchers, educators, and clinicians have routinely assumed that a child's spontaneous answers represent what the child is able to think and actually does think and believe. What if researchers took as much genuine interest in the actual experience of children as we think parents should take? Would they discover more than they had expected?

> INTERVIEWER: Is the moon alive?
> CHILD: Yes, it is.
> INTERVIEWER: How do you know?
> CHILD: Because it follows me when I walk.
> INTERVIEWER: How do you know it follows you?
> CHILD: Because when I move, it moves.
> INTERVIEWER: So, when you get home, it follows you right into your house through the door?
> CHILD: No! It doesn't come inside.
> INTERVIEWER: It doesn't? Why not?
> CHILD: Because it *can't* come inside. Not really, silly!

This interviewer is genuinely interested in children. In fact, she has a lot of fun talking with children. In this sense, she's much more like Art Linkletter, Bill Cosby, or Rosie O'Donnell than Bruno Bettelheim or Jean Piaget. And she certainly didn't accept the child's categorical answer at face value. Instead, she kept probing. And, as is often the case, she didn't have to probe very much. She quickly discovered that this young child was nowhere near as naïve and gullible as the traditional experts think.

Realistic Child Development Research

Well over half a century of realistic child development research has shown that beneath the superficial appearance of what we call "spontaneous childhood behavioral style" lies a much more complex and sophisticated being than is hinted at by the developmental model that reigns in the world of contemporary American education and mental health. Over fifty years ago, in 1945, the psychologists I. Huang and H. W. Lee explained that animism is the result of an overgeneralization. Children may say an object is "alive" and yet refuse to attribute any properties of life to it. When push comes to shove, children actually know the difference.

Contemporary child development researchers like Margaret Donaldson of the University of Edinburgh and Rochel Gelman of UCLA have shown that when Piaget's developmental tasks are put into contexts that make sense to young children—i.e., when children are the object of interest, not the model and the tasks—even preschoolers can be infinitely more competent than the model of the child as seen by the education and mental health establishments would suggest. Other developmentalists such as Henry M. Wellman of the University of Michigan, Janet Astington of the University of Toronto's Ontario Institute for Studies in Education, and Paul L. Harris of the University of Oxford have demonstrated in many elegant experiments that children as young as two and a half are developing a complex *theory of mind* that allows them to understand the perspectives, motives, intent, and reasoning of others. Psychologists such as Esther Thelen and Linda B. Smith of Indiana University have shown that even infants can use experience to develop skills that were described as impossible by traditional Piagetian theory and research and as yet-to-come by contemporary maturationist brain function models. Finally, researchers such as Barry Parsonson and Kathleen Naughton of New Zealand's Waikato University have shown that some cognitive skills traditionally believed to develop between the ages of eleven and fifteen can be taught in mere minutes to five-year-olds and that the "invariant order" in which these cognitive skills supposedly had to be learned could be reversed. When all is said and done, children turn out to be complex, sophisticated, and realistic *at the very same time that they are vulnerable to the literal meaning of words and to the consequences of reasoning logically without the benefit of the perspective conferred by extensive experience.*

Bad Butterflies Can Be Real but Kids Know
That the Moon's Not Alive

Now, can the same child who could accurately tell his interviewer (if questioned extensively enough in a child-friendly manner) that the moon isn't really alive still be terrified by "bad butterflies"? Absolutely. By the time a child is four or five, experience has already taught him that while the moon *seems* to move when he moves, it never actually shows up in any of the places where he hangs out. The four- to six-year-old already understands that he and the moon exist in very different spaces. The bad-butterflies experience, however, is of an entirely different nature. Children much older than two-and-a-half-year-olds are not immune. The intense realness of such experiences wipes away any developing perspective the child may have begun to acquire. As we saw, it will require new experience to resolve the old experience.

Children Can Only Predict What Experience Allows

"One assumption" [that young children make], Tufts psychologist David Elkind tells us, "is that the world is purposeful, that everything has a purpose or cause, and that there is no possibility of chance or arbitrary events." Elkind is not alone in this belief, for it is still the common wisdom of a world of child experts. Indeed, the same Piagetian developmental model that assured us that young children see the world in animistic terms also tells us that they believe that living things like trees are intentional and can do things on purpose. After all, young children certainly do seem to talk and behave as if they believed these things! That's why, the experts say, four-year-old Stuart can claim with complete sincerity that the tree he was climbing "made him fall." The branch Stuart was sitting on didn't break accidentally. No, the tree made him fall on purpose. Stuart, the experts say, simply can't understand at this stage in his life what an accident is.

Let's rethink this whole issue from the child's perspective and see if the experts are right.

First of all, what is an accident? An *accident is an unpredictable event that occurs independently.* In other words, an accident is something that no one can foresee and that no one caused on purpose. This means that at any moment, in any place, anything could happen. *Any* branch could break. *Any* tree could fall. *Any* wing could break. *Any* car could go out of control. *Any* dam could burst. *Any* house could catch on fire. Lightning could strike *anywhere*. And all of these things can happen at *any* time without *any* warning whatsoever.

What's a little mind supposed to do with the ever-present threat of uncaused and unpredictable events? After all, a completely unpredictable world is not a livable world!

The young child has only two real choices. He can either be paralyzed by fear because the very next moment may bring disaster, or he can conveniently redefine reality in order to make life more livable. And that's exactly what young children do. They redefine the world. The world can be made a whole lot safer if *that particular tree* is seen as a "bad" tree. Just avoid the bad tree and you're okay!

Only Experience Can Put Things in Perspective

Why aren't adults paralyzed by their knowledge of the accidental? Because years and years of experience has taught us that, while common in the world, accidents are uncommon in the lives of any given individual. We know the automobile and airplane accident statistics. We're always hearing about these things on the nightly news. And yet most people still drive and fly without being paralyzed by fear. Long experience tells us that it's reasonably safe to do so.

But how do we know that it is really experience, and not just factual knowledge, that brings us our sense of safety, security, and predictability? Because our sense of safety, security, and predictability can be profoundly shattered by just one experience. All it takes is just one bad accident—or any bad experience that we view as "traumatic"—and our whole sense of the reliability of the world can be undermined.

Once it's shattered, how do adults regain their sense of safety, security, and predictability, the overall feeling that the world is a reliable place? Does it work to tell an adult who has just had a horrible car accident that the statistical likelihood of having another accident is very low? Of course not. Instead, assuming that they're physically fit to drive, we try to get them back behind the wheel as quickly as possible. We know that the longer the person takes to drive again, the harder it will be. *Only experi-*

ence can help reconstitute the safety and reliability of the world. While the form may differ, there's really no substantial difference between getting the car accident victim back behind the wheel and using our special magic spray to get rid of bad butterflies. Each creates a correcting experience that is appropriate for the individual's life context.

Children's Experience of Space and Time Is Different

Every adult knows that the older you get the more quickly time seems to pass. In fact, that's one of the reasons why adults look back on childhood with longing and envy. Space, too, has an entirely different feel in childhood. And the world of childhood is infinitely smaller and infinitely richer. Under what we narrowly think of as "normal" circumstances, the world of childhood is also infinitely safer. Absent the TV nightly news and newspaper headlines, Bosnia, Croatia, and Kosovo don't even exist, and school shootings are unimaginable.

When the small world of childhood is upset by scary things, parents often fail to realize that the words they use to reassure may be meaningless to their child.

For example, when a five-year-old asks her mother, "Are there any volcanoes around here?" it is easy for her mother to recognize her daughter's worry about what might happen if there were (although she might not realize how realistic the TV ads were that advertised the volcano movie). But when that same mother says, "Don't worry. The closest volcano is over two thousand miles away," she may not be as reassuring as she thinks she is. Because parents rarely think about such things, the five-year-old's mother is not likely to realize that "two thousand miles" is still an empty expression for her daughter. This is true even for children, like her daughter, who have a rather amazing ability to talk about practically anything. Had her mother said, "Don't worry, sweetie, it would take us at least six days by car, driving all day long, before we even got close to one!" her daughter would have had a more realistic sense of just how far away the volcanoes really were.

Experience Changes Meaning

Five-year-old Philip had developed a horrible fear of the bathtub. He would become extremely anxious and agitated as bathtime approached and then he would be literally terrified of getting into the tub. In the weeks that followed, Philip's fears began to spill over into the rest of the day in the form of an unfamiliar anxiety that his mom found most disturbing.

Like many mothers, Philip's mom reads lots of magazines and watches a lot of television. So she thought that she knew the signs of the onset of a child psychiatric disorder. To reassure herself that she was on the right track, she made a beeline to her favorite megabookstore and purchased the latest books on childhood disorders. Sure enough, Philip's behavior corresponded perfectly to Childhood Anxiety Disorder.

Her suspicion reinforced, she made and kept an appointment with a child psychiatrist. She was relieved to have her suspicion confirmed that her son suffered from a very common childhood psychiatric disorder. She was saddened, but not surprised, to learn that her child also had a lifelong brain-based disorder of probable genetic origin. She was disappointed that the treatment would probably have to last as long as the disorder itself, but at least she was glad that there was a simple solution in the form of medication.

It Helps to Know Something About Children

What's missing from the all-too-common story of Philip and his mother? The answer: Philip. Neither Philip's mom nor his new child psychiatrist looked for a simple explanation of the acute and unexpected onset of Philip's bath anxiety. After all, that's where it had all begun—in the bathroom.

Adults assume that all experience is basically the same. This is why the sudden onset of Philip's anxiety over something as familiar, mundane, and banal as the bathtub *must* signal the onset of a disorder of "internal" origin. There's just no reason why a familiar bathtub should suddenly provoke uncontrollable anxiety in a child who has bathed in it comfortably for years.

But that's not how meaning works for any of us, let alone for young children.

Until the onset of Philip's anxiety, bathtubs were places where you washed up and had fun playing with all sorts of water toys. And until he had started taking swimming lessons six weeks earlier, Philip didn't have a clue what drowning was. But what we saw once we looked carefully was that suddenly Philip had realized that *you can drown in a bathtub!* Now we can understand what happened to him and make sense out of his "meaningless" anxiety that supposedly arose directly from his genetically primed brain.

Change the Present and You Change the Past

Philip's experience is neither unusual nor extreme. These are the sorts of everyday meaning changes that we all experience. The difference is that, in childhood, the consequences of such abrupt meaning changes can be cataclysmic.

Over the years, many parents we have worked with have complained that something that their child "has always known" couldn't possibly be the cause of present problems. Parents assume that meaning remains the same over time. In Philip's case, meaning changed because of new information, new knowledge. However, meaning can also change for developmental reasons as well. Children go through periods when their ability to perceive fine detail and to recognize subtle meanings and subtle interrelationships undergoes a burst of complexity. Our experience has taught us that many children undergo such a burst at about five years of age.

At these moments, it is not just the child's present that becomes more complex. It is the past as well.

One of the most common examples of profound but subtle meaning change can be seen in the experience of children of single parents. Many mothers we have worked with over the years have said that they found it difficult to believe that not having a father around could play much of a role in the present problems because their child had grown up comfortably without one. As it happens, the huge increase in the child's ability to understand complex meaning and interrelationships often coincides with starting kindergarten or first grade. While the child may have previously attended preschool, where he was exposed to many other children, often the beginning of regular school offers the first real chance to engage in after-school activities in which parents may be involved. Thus a child who was previously comfortable with a single parent may find himself exposed for the first time on a regular basis to two-parent families. New realizations bring new questions, which, in turn, require answers. Because children often act out questions rather than ask them out loud, their behavior may appear to undergo strange changes. And as the young child begins to fill in the blanks created by the comparisons and questions, he can come to all sorts of conclusions that lead to further complications. As one young child once said to us, "A dad wouldn't leave a good kid, so it must have been my fault"—a perfectly logical, if untrue, conclusion. There are as many variations on these historical rewrite themes as there are children and families.

Listen Carefully and Explore

Perhaps you're a bit overwhelmed by the detail and complexity of even very young children's thinking and by how easily they are misled by words and experiences. If so, that's understandable. But there's no reason to become overly concerned. And the good news is that the best thing you can do about all this is simply to get to know your child.

Listen carefully to what you and others say. Once you really become attuned to the logic of language, the world will never look or sound the same again. You'll begin to hear things you've never heard and to see potentially troubling situations you never even thought existed. This will allow you many, many opportunities to clarify your child's understandings and interpretations of experience.

Knowing that there are reasons why children react to everyday experiences the way they do also decreases the likelihood that you will rush to mistaken psychiatric explanations and mistreatments for what are often easily solved problems. In any case, the more sensitive you become to these issues, the richer your understanding of your child's experience can be. And the richer your understanding of your child's experience is, the richer your relationship can become.

6

Pay Attention!

"Hey, Nick, could you not climb on there, please?" the mom at the fast-food restaurant asks matter-of-factly as her four- or five-year-old begins to move from his standing position on the bench beside her to the top of a neighboring table. "You're going to get hurt," the mom continues between bites, "and you know it, too!" This monologue continues in a now perfectly predictable manner until the mom finishes her last bite and tells Nick's little sister to hurry up because she's had it and they're leaving. The mom piles Nick's barely touched cheeseburger and fries onto the tray, empties the tray into the trash, and the three make a hasty exit. "No, THIS way," we hear the mom say as the three approach the exit. "Don't you ever pay attention!"

This scene or one of its countless variations is repeated millions of times a day. The result is chronically smoldering frustration punctuated by moments of exasperated anger as many millions of parents conclude that their children literally can't pay attention.

But if you look to the traditional sources of information on why children don't pay attention, you'll find yourself on a wild goose chase that leads only to all sorts of would-be "brain-based" attentional disorders like Attention Deficit Disorder (ADD) and its variant Attention Deficit–Hyperactivity Disorder (ADHD). Once again, we think you'll learn much more just by listening carefully and consciously and by thinking about what's actually going on when you interact and communicate.

Logical Thinking Doesn't
Have to Be Conscious

It's easy to see the logic of language at work when children fear "bad ducks" and don't want their fathers to "put them to sleep." But there are times when the logic of language is much harder to recognize. This is when logic works so quickly and so completely that the process is entirely unconscious. Every parent has experienced these moments, but very few, if any, recognize that the very same logic is at work. Here's an exchange that many parents with teens or younger children have experienced in one form or another:

> Jack's mother opens the door to his bedroom and sees Jack sitting mesmerized in front of the TV screen, frenetically pressing buttons on his Nintendo controller.
>
> "Jack," Mother says, "how many times have I told you to *clean up this room*!" Jack continues zapping away. "Do you have any idea what your father is going to do when he gets home!" Jack looks up vaguely between shots at the oncoming creature. "I WANT IT CLEAN BY SIX!" Jack's mother practically screams in order to make herself heard. Shortly before six, Jack's mother returns to find Jack in exactly the same spot as when she left. The room hasn't been touched. When she finally gets his attention, Jack's mother says, "I told you to clean up your room."
>
> "No, you didn't!"
>
> "Yes, I did."
>
> "No, YOU DIDN'T!"
>
> "Yes, I most certainly did! Not only did I tell you to clean it up, I told you *three times* and I told you to have it done by six!"

By now it should be more than obvious that if Jack's mother really meant to tell her son to clean up his room, she certainly didn't say what she meant. But there's more to what happened here than just ineffective parent communication style. What actually flashed through Jack's mind in response to what his mother said to him?

MOM: "How many times have I told you to *clean up this room!*"
JACK: "Who knows—five, ten, twenty!"

MOM: "Do you have any idea what your father is going to do when he gets home!"
JACK: "Yep. Same thing he always does . . ."

MOM: "I WANT IT CLEAN BY SIX!"
JACK: "So what!"

The significance of the fact that Jack's mother asked two questions and expressed one desire is not just that she didn't say what she really meant. What is new here is our understanding of the fact that *each of the things Jack's mom said, each utterance, could be logically satisfied by the most superficial response.* Under such circumstances, no conscious awareness of the content is required. The whole process occurred automatically—as if his mother tapped his knee with a doctor's reflex hammer. Question in, answer out. Poof! All over in a flash with no conscious awareness whatsoever.

Isn't This a Dumb Way to Design Thinking?

Why would Nature provide us with the means NOT to know what's going on?

Actually, being able to respond automatically and mechanically is really a very efficient way of making sure that we are free to attend to those things in life that really do require conscious attention. It also allows us to do many things, often very different things, at the same time. If we had to be consciously aware of everything we think or do, life would be reduced to a series of millions of individual microdecisions. We wouldn't have time for anything else. The classic act of walking, talking, and chewing gum simultaneously would be an impossible challenge. And activities requiring complex motor skills and strategic thinking like sports—everything from table tennis to basketball—would be out of the question.

Besides what the computer world calls multitasking—the ability to accomplish different tasks at the same time—evolution has equipped us with the ability to deal categorically with categorical input. Most of the time, this setup is quite efficient. But sometimes, as Jack and his mom illustrate so well, it can be counterproductive.

Communication Styles and Conscious Awareness

When we act and/or think without being aware of what we're thinking or doing, both the content and process of thinking and doing are said to be *dissociated* from conscious awareness.

Dissociation

Whenever you do something automatically—such as putting away the items you were carrying when you came home and then not remembering either putting them away or where you put them—you have *dissociated the experience*. It was split off from your conscious awareness. We don't lay down memory of automatic and mechanical thoughts or acts because they're outside of conscious awareness in the first place.

The most striking common example of dissociation is "highway amnesia," being so wrapped up in what you're thinking that you're not aware of driving and can't remember any of the trip once you arrive at your destination. It's not that you've repressed the memory of your drive. It's just that your thoughts were elsewhere.

Communication Styles and Dissociation

Certain communication styles promote the automatic mechanical processing of what is communicated, making it much more likely that content will never make it into conscious awareness. We actually coined a term for such styles: *dissociogenic*.

Dissociation, automatic behavior, and *amnesia* are psychiatric terms that pop up when you read about child abuse, psychological trauma, and bizarre conditions such as Multiple Personality Disorder. They don't seem something the average parent needs to know about, but dissociogenic communication styles are much more common than you might think and play a much larger role in the everyday problems of parents and children than anyone realizes.

Dissociation and Lying in Young Children

The most often-quoted, established definition of clinical dissociation is from Frank Putnam's book on Multiple Personality Disorder: "Dissociative states are characterized by significant alterations in the integrative functions of memory for thoughts, feelings, or actions, and significant alterations in sense of self."

This may sound complicated, but it is actually something that every parent has seen over and over again.

Imagine catching your five-year-old with his hand literally in the cookie jar. "No, I didn't eat those cookies," he protests, his face still covered with crumbs. To appreciate the dissociative nature of his response, you must realize that, at the very moment of the denial, your son neither remembers that he ate the cookie nor tastes the cookie that is still in his mouth.

As far-fetched as it may seem, when your little boy protests that he didn't eat those cookies, *he's not lying.* A lie is a conscious twisting of the truth in an effort to deceive. Even though his face is covered with crumbs and there's still half-chewed cookie in his mouth, he is absolutely sincere in his denial. (Keep this in mind for the future. Sincerity is not a virtue.

Sincerity is simply a belief in what is said. Sincerity can be immensely misleading.) When very young children maintain the opposite of what is clearly the case, they are redefining their own reality, something that is very different than the conscious, purposeful intent to deceive another person. Somewhere around two to two and a half years of age, children learn to understand the intentions of others—and also become capable of deception themselves.

Most parents, however, don't buy the denial or the claim of what appears to be very convenient amnesia. When a child says, instantly upon knocking the lamp off the end table, "I didn't break that lamp" the immediacy of the event and the denial make it hard to believe that the protest is anything but a lie. Yet it's not. It's too instantaneous, too automatic, and too mechanical. Does this mean that the same child is incapable of lying at this point in development? Not at all. It just means that dissociating and lying are two very different things.

This distinction is extremely important, because if you treat automatic mechanical reflex-like responses as purposeful conscious acts, you will be overcomplicating the situation and inviting an indignant denial, which nearly always leads to a huge standoff. When this happens, arguments stretch out, fights erupt, egos get bruised, and pride demands a defense.

While dissociative responses are common throughout childhood and adolescence, they tend to peak around age five and again during adolescence. The vehemence with which adolescents can deny the obvious can be quite intense. By recognizing these automatic and mechanical reactions for what they are, you can spare yourself immense grief and frustration simply by avoiding pointless fights over what's true and what's not.

The Double Whammy

Empty questions, as we've said, are dissociogenic because they can be dismissed instantaneously with an automatic mechanical response, but *negative questions* are potentially even more self-defeating. Think about the following examples:

- Don't you want to go to the store with me?
- Don't you want to sit on Mommy's lap?

- Can't you just do what you're told?
- Can't you remember to clean up your room?

Not only is each of these questions ineffective because it doesn't say what the parent means, each is a negative suggestion. Each question introduces the notion of *doubt*. To see what the potential logical impact of each question is, just turn it around and make it into a statement:

- You don't want to go to the store with me.
- You don't want to sit on Mommy's lap.
- You can't just do what you're told.
- You can't remember to clean up your room.

The Double Whammy is the combination of an empty statement or question that can be dismissed without conscious awareness or the "appropriate" response PLUS an implicit negative statement and the introduction of doubt. Again, not exactly what parents really want to do! It's a bit like saying to a child "You don't really want to do what I told you to do and you can't remember it anyway!"

So what's the antidote? It's simple: Just don't use questions, negative questions, and empty statements. Say clearly what you mean and mean exactly what you say.

Isn't This Just Like Hypnosis?

You may have thought you noticed a certain similarity between the dissociative, automatic behavior we're discussing and what we routinely think of as hypnosis. Well, you're not off the mark. *A suggestion becomes "hypnotic" when a person acts in accordance with the suggestion without being aware of doing so.* This means that parents are routinely engaging in behaviors that have everything in common with trance induction and various hypnotic techniques. Is it any wonder that so many parents complain about their children being "zoned out" when:

- Every question creates the opportunity for an automatic mechanical response without awareness

- Negative questions introduce doubt and suggest the very opposite of what the parent intends
- Repeated questions further reinforce automatic, mechanical, unconscious nonresponsiveness without behavioral compliance
- Each repeated question *or command* suggests that the child didn't hear, didn't register, or didn't understand the first and subsequent questions or commands. This trains children to tune out questions or commands altogether or not to "hear" them until a certain threshold has been reached. The average child doesn't believe that his parent really means it until the fourth or fifth time.

Once again, the antidote to this mess is, first and foremost, to recognize that there are self-defeating features built into our everyday communication styles. We're not talking about "communication disorders" or "speech and language pathology." You don't need a specialist. We're talking about everyday language. But it's hard to say what you mean and mean what you say if you're not aware of how everyday language complicates your life.

Everyday Zombie Experiences

But there's even more. Anyone who has ever played video games knows that they can be intensely absorbing. When our attention is absorbed by one activity, it is withdrawn from all others. At such times, we're *wrapped up* in what we're doing, which means that we can't see or hear through the "wrapping." When Jack's mom opened his bedroom door and saw him all wrapped up in his zap-'em-blow-'em-up Nintendo game, she should have realized that his attention was not available. Jack was in another universe, as far as the rest of the world was concerned. So, yes, indeed, she may just as well have been talking to the wall!

Jack's mom thought that she had gained her son's attention when he looked up fleetingly or when he said, "Okay!" in response to "I WANT IT CLEAN BY SIX!" But all Jack's mom really got was a reflex response. No attention and no conscious awareness were required for Jack's Nintendo-ized brain to zap out the stock reply to a stock statement.

Commanding Attention

Our part of Florida has the second-highest incidence of pedestrian accidents of anywhere in the country, and bike riders are also frequent victims of unwanted encounters with motorized vehicles. One of our retired friends, who gets around mostly on bicycle, learned a lesson that could have benefited Jack's mother.

"You know," he told us, "I thought it was safe to keep going across the street because the driver looked right at me. It was when he turned the corner anyway and ran me down that I realized that, although he had looked right at me, he hadn't seen me."

What was the lesson of our friend's broken leg and painfully long convalescence? "When you want someone's attention, *make sure that they actually see you* and not just look in your direction."

The highway amnesia phenomenon tells us that driving and video games have some things in common. Both can be intensely dissociogenic. If you're a pedestrian or a bike rider crossing the street, you obviously can't get in the approaching car and tap the driver on the shoulder. But that's what it may take—literally—when children are wrapped up in Nintendo-like activities or are absorbed in trancelike spacing out. Just touch the child's shoulder or gently put your hand on their arm. The physical contact, plus speaking, will usually disrupt the intense concentration. At this point, communication starts to become possible.

Many Everyday Activities Are Dissociogenic

Some experiences are more intensely dissociogenic than others. Any activity that requires focused attention can induce dissociation. Add intensity and repetitiveness and the activity can become even more absorbing. Finally, add duration—stretch the activity out over time—and it can become trancelike. Dissociation can heighten efficiency and productivity, as anyone who has ever worked on an assembly line knows, but it does so at a price. It disconnects the individual from the rest of his environment. And, as assembly line workers know, sometimes it takes a while to reconnect with the world you have so successfully shut out.

Some young children rock back and forth purposefully in order to go into a trance, to dissociate and withdraw from the world. Some children discover rocking simply in the course of experience. Others who are fearful or troubled by some aspect of the world may actually develop rocking as a successful way of putting their thoughts elsewhere. Lots of children rock themselves to sleep at night. Other self-stimulating activities, well known to parents, include thumb-sucking and rubbing the face with fuzz from a blanket. Some children combine all three—rocking, thumb-sucking, and rhythmic fuzz rubbing.

As we all know, intense absorption can be quite pleasurable. Or at least it can be quite unpleasant to be brought out of an intensely focused state. So these states tend to become self-perpetuating.

None of these activities are "pathological" in and of themselves. Thumb-sucking should be discouraged simply because it can deform the oral cavity, necessitating expensive and inconvenient braces later on. If rocking persists well into the preschool years, it may prompt complaints or concern from preschool staff. And other self-stimulatory activities will also be seen as signs of immaturity if not frank disturbance. If these spontaneous self-hypnotizing behaviors persist, it may become more difficult to promote productive attention, so it makes sense to interrupt them gently by offering alternatives. With a young child, you can say—again, gently, of course—"Don't rock. Just go to sleep" and perhaps spend a few more minutes at your child's bedside. You can also make reading a bedtime story contingent on not rocking or sucking. But do so in a way that facilitates your goal, not in a way that sets up a power struggle. Be matter-of-fact and give 100 percent credit for every bit of cooperation. By taking such an approach, and by combining it with the other basic communication and interaction approaches we discuss later, in chapter 8, you can decrease these self-stimulatory dissociative behaviors while promoting attention and connectedness.

7

Now You Hear It, Now You Don't

Family Secrets

Secrets are a normal and necessary part of life. They can also make life enjoyable, as when parents secretly provide Santa's presents or the Easter Bunny's candy eggs. Having an absolutarian attitude toward secrets and honesty can actually kill much of the magic of childhood. Parents needn't worry that such secret-keeping promotes dishonesty, because children treat such secrets very differently than they do common everyday confidences. Children are immensely protective of their own developmental needs and, to the extent that adults will allow it, the wonder, mystery, and naïveté of childhood.

Open and Closed Secrets

There are two basic types of secrets—open and closed. A closed secret is one of which the other person has absolutely no knowledge. Closed secrets can have an effect on you and your life, but that's all. For instance, if your parent secretly withheld money that could be used, say, for your education, you would miss out on many opportunities, but your ignorance of the deception would protect you from any further confusion and pain. Closed secrets can't affect your thinking. They don't "play" with your mind.

Open secrets are another matter entirely. Imagine that you enter a room where a person—say, a very special person such as a parent—is sitting at a table. As you approach the table, your parent slowly and subtly moves his right hand over to an object, which he removes from sight (covers it up, slips it into a drawer, etc.). This is an open secret. The "secret" act is literally right out in the open.

What does an open secret demand of you?

> You saw me hide the object.
>> But you're *not supposed to see* what I did.
>> And you're *not supposed to know* what I did.
>> And you're *not supposed to know that you know* what I did.

To make it even more complicated,

> You're *not supposed to know that I know that you know* what I did.
>> And you're *not supposed to know that I know that you know that I know that you know* what I did.

How Common Are Open Secrets?

They are amazingly common! First of all, adults routinely treat children, especially young children, as if they didn't understand 90 percent of what goes on around them. We've been amazed to see that even our colleagues—psychologists, psychiatrists, and child therapists—act as if children are oblivious to much of their own experience. Parents routinely forget their child is present when talking with other adults in person or on the phone. Like everyone else, parents get lost in what they're doing and forget where they are and who's around. Or they fool themselves into thinking that they're communicating nothing to their children by using "code" that is easily deciphered by the average four-year-old.

We routinely tell the families we work with that *when we see three-year-olds, we assume that they know all the family secrets.* And most of the time, we're right. Here are a few open secrets that we've encountered clinically.

- Parents who divorced for practical reasons (taxes, etc.) and never told the children
- Previously married parents who assume that they've never disclosed the fact
- Families in which an aunt or a grandmother is really the child's biological mother
- Families in which a child from a previous marriage is not supposed to notice that she has no physical similarity to her brothers and sisters
- Children who were born (often long) before their parents were married
- Families in which an obvious illness goes unacknowledged
- Families in which one child has a different last name than his brothers and sisters
- Families in which parents argue or fight bitterly but discord is not acknowledged
- Families where an absent parent contributes nothing to the children but "normal" relations are maintained
- Families in which a stepparent—usually a stepfather—is "such a good parent" but has a horrible or nonexistent relationship with a child or children from a previous marriage

Open Secrets Are Dissociogenic

Open secrets require self-crippling mental gymnastics on the part of the human mind. Many of the families with open secrets that we have seen over the years have children who do poorly in school and who have often been identified as "learning disabled." Why? Just think about what school is. In the simplest of terms, *school is a place where children tell adults what they know*—through oral work, written work, and classroom behavior. A family secret represents knowledge of which the child cannot even be aware that he is aware.

This simple but bizarre situation created by an open secret requires a whole new style of "knowing" in which the obvious simply isn't dealt with. It effectively requires children to tune out and fail to understand the obvious. Over time, these patterns become relatively stable cognitive-behavioral styles.

This makes it very hard for perfectly normal children to tell adults—teachers, in this case—what they know. As a result, these children do poorly academically even though it's obvious to everyone that they *ought* to know the answers. (This is, after all, the "IQ/performance discrepancy" definition of "learning disabilities.")

It Doesn't All Add Up, So Forget It!

There are many variations on the family-secret theme. In one of the first cases that we saw together, Gina, a ten-year-old girl with "documented developmental dyscalculalia"—a math disability—was brought because of oppositional-defiant behavior, aggressiveness, and social isolation. Mother and Gina were look-alikes with strawberry blond hair and fair complexions. Dad and younger sister were very dark and very Mediterranean in appearance. During the first play encounter, Gina said nonchalantly, "My parents have the nicest wedding album, but, you know, I've never been able to figure out why the flowers in front of the church—which only bloom in the fall—were blooming in the spring." Debbie handed her a piece of paper and a pencil and asked, "How long does it take to make a baby?" Within a few minutes, Gina had figured out that she had to have been at least fifteen months old when her parents were married.

Gina's "math disability" disappeared instantaneously.

What Happens When You Can't Access What You Know?

In computer terms, you could have the world's most powerful and fastest processor, the biggest and fastest hard drive, and the finest, most up-to-date software available. But if you can't access your RAM, your random access memory, then you can't utilize all that marvelous hardware and software. And that's just what open secrets do. They can turn perfectly observant, intelligent people into functionally handicapped thinkers.

And, to make matters even more complicated, the open secret does not need to be "serious." In fact, it can be quite innocuous. It's not the seriousness of the secret itself that does the damage. It's the fact that secrets prevent us from accessing what we know—which keeps us from using our good minds. Open secrets prevent us from dealing with something that is right in front of our noses.

"Yes, But I Don't Think She Really Knows"

Most parents are quite convinced that they're good at keeping secrets. Parents also think they're quite adept at choosing private places to confide in each other or that they're masters of some sort of verbal Morse code that can't be deciphered by anyone who isn't already well into adolescence. So you can imagine the look of utter shock (and often embarrassment) on parents' faces when Debbie returns from the playtherapy room with a secret that the parents swear that their child "couldn't *possibly* know!" And yet he or she does—often in great detail.

Knowledge, like memory of specific events or experiences, need not be conscious. So many children we have seen over the years had no conscious awareness at all that they were in possession of family secrets. Yet once their attention was drawn specifically to this issue, most of their parents didn't find it hard to see that the secret knowledge was implicit in their child's behavior, attitudes, and/or relationships.

It's not uncommon for a parent who calls up for an initial appointment to say immediately that a particular subject is off limits and should not be broached during the intake interview because the child is not yet aware of it. Nearly every time, we've been able to demonstrate to the calling parent that the forbidden knowledge is implicit in the very problem behavior they describe. When this is the case, we warn the parent that since the supposed secret is already part of the problem they want to solve, we won't be able to help them unless we can deal openly with the very secret they don't want discussed. If they insist on keeping a "secret" that is clearly already known to the child, we decline the case because we would be absolutely useless to the child as well as to the family. While some parents who agree to deal frankly with open secrets do have some rocky moments after the secret is acknowledged and discussed openly, most find that it is much less difficult to deal openly with what everyone already knows than to maintain the precarious cognitive and emotional balancing act required by the secret.

8

How to Avoid the ADHD Trap
by Using Communication to Shape
Your Child's Attentional Style

Parents Often Misinterpret Automatic
Thinking as a "Brain Disorder"

Jack's mother's first and very understandable reaction to her Nintendo-playing son's defiant insistence that she never once told him to clean up his room is to be hurt by the fact that her son has so little respect for his parents and authority. But with repeated experiences like their misunderstanding over cleaning up his room, Jack's mom may very logically (!) conclude that Jack simply doesn't register what she and others say, so there must therefore be something inherently wrong with Jack's brain.

This misunderstanding of a basic human cognitive-behavioral style is probably the most common origin for the epidemic of "receptive language disorders" and "central processing disorders" that are believed to be plaguing American children today. And since education and mental health professionals are only people like Jack's mom, their communication styles are not likely to be any more effective than hers. So we can imagine what the official results will be: the beginning of a lifelong formal "disability" that will never respond to "appropriate treatment" because it was never anything other than a normal human cognitive-behavioral style in the first place.

If you take the trouble to read the authoritative works on "developmental speech and language disorders," you will be surprised to find that "the experts"—teachers, counselors, pediatricians, psychologists, and psychiatrists—routinely engage in exactly the same counterproductive and dissociogenic behaviors parents do! These things are initially hard to recognize simply because they are so "normal." They're overly familiar, a part of our everyday life. The tragedy is that the failure of adults to understand how children think and what words do results in the misdiagnosis, mislabeling, miseducation, and mistreatment of millions of children.

Attentional Styles

A person's attentional style is just one of many cognitive-behavioral styles. Like temperament, many of these styles are recognizable very early in life. Although some cognitive-behavioral styles may be resistant to change, *you should always assume that any behavior is potentially changeable* until proven otherwise.

Spontaneous Attenders and Space Kids

Some children seem to be natural-born Spontaneous Attenders. They seem tuned in to their environment and attentive to change from the very beginning. You don't have to work hard to gain and keep their attention and they need little reminding. As they get older, the Spontaneous Attenders also tend to stick with activities longer even if they're not of the greatest interest to the child. These children tend to complete tasks, spend more time in productive studying, etc. Their ability to focus and persevere is often accompanied by a more robust frustration-tolerance.

On the other hand, Space Kids seem out of touch and space out easily and often. These children seem less tuned-in to their environment. While less attentive to change, they may tolerate less well the changes and transitions life demands of them. You often have to make more of an effort to gain and keep their attention, and they need lots of reminding. As they approach the school years, Space Kids need more prompting and structure. Learning how to study is more of a task for them. Space Kids' frustration tolerance is often lower than the Spontaneous Attenders'.

Diversity, Not Pathology

These two ends of the attention spectrum do NOT represent health and pathology. They represent another aspect of life's extraordinary diversity, variations on a highly complex theme. Space Kids do not need to be "fixed" because they're not "broken." They will, however, require more of your attention.

Shaping Attentional Styles

If parents realized how much they can do to shape even difficult and resistant attentional styles, we wouldn't be experiencing our current national epidemic of formal attentional disorders. As it stands, adults are so convinced that they themselves have no power to shape the attentional styles of children that children as young as one year of age are being diagnosed with Attention Deficit–Hyperactivity Disorder and being "treated" with a variety of medications including lithium, Prozac and other antidepressants, clonidine, and stimulants like Ritalin and Dexedrine!

Visit any part of the world that has not succumbed to America's conviction that 25 percent of its population is formally disabled and you will see mothers—uninstructed, uneducated, and unsophisticated in their knowledge of childhood disorders—who routinely externally modulate their babies' biobehavioral states. These mothers facilitate their babies' transitions from one biobehavioral state to another, soothing, calming, and *focusing their babies' attention.* Not only can this be done, it is done—routinely—by millions of mothers.

Common Things Occur Commonly

Before opting for unnecessary diagnosis and treatment "solutions," the first thing to realize is that we live in a spastic, disconnected, fractionated world that encourages separateness and self-absorption. This Nintendo-ized channel-surfing world full of instant foods and meal substitutes discourages almost everything that takes time, energy, and old-fashioned concentration—stick-to-it-iveness. Who needs to learn how to prepare a good meal when the fridge and the microwave are handy? Who needs to read a book or compose a well-thought-out essay when the electronic version of those old printed crib notes allows you to cut and paste and never write an original word? Who needs to learn how to get along with other children when you can spend entire days and nights mesmerized in front of the video screen? And why read at all when you can get instant gratification from increasingly realistic multimedia?

The Antidote to One Style
Is Another Style

Fortunately, it's not necessary for parents to fix the world, although they may have to restrict it a bit. All parents really need to do is to play with, have fun with, talk to, and listen to their children. The best way parents can shape even longstanding attentional styles is with another style.

Because this sounds "too simple," it's all too easy to dismiss. And yet that's exactly what owners do with pets. When we (firmly but gently) housebreak a dog or train a dog to behave a certain way in public, we create an interactive behavioral style of our own that we use to shape the animal's behavior. Since animals like dogs, cats, and horses don't understand language the way even a twelve-month-old does, it's not all the nice things that people say to pets that result in successful training. It's the patterned style with which the pet owner relates to his pet that gets the results. So don't underestimate the formative power of "mere" behavior when it comes to complex children.

Focus Attention by Sharing It

When you play with your infant—simple things like peek-a-boo—you are focusing and shaping attention. And you are beginning to teach your child how to engage in *joint attention*. Many parents, excited to have a new being in their life, enjoy these first joint activities. And then they stop, wrapped up in other things competing for their time. As soon as the baby becomes coordinated enough to manipulate objects, and the parent becomes busy enough to need to do other things, solitary activities begin to replace the lovely joint activities that actually shape attentional and relating styles.

You are doing the most important thing you can do when you simply engage in joint activities with your child. Start reading to your child early, but don't expect her to learn how to read from this joint process. That's not the goal (although it is the best way to get there). The initial goal is simply to foster your child's attention within a sharing relationship. So don't worry if your child seems more interested in the illustrations than in the story. Just keep sharing. Every cooperative project carried to some sort of completion promotes focused attention, continuity of experience, and a natural sense of completion. And since our multimedia world seems designed to disrupt continuous experience, the everyday sharing of activities between parent and child works to counter this trend.

Focus Attention by Recognizing the Fear of Failure

We have discovered over the years that the vast majority of children referred to us for ADD can attend perfectly well. If you were to watch these children, mostly boys, through the one-way mirror into our playtherapy room, you would see absolutely classic ADD behavior as these children flit from one thing to another. But if you looked carefully and didn't accept their behavior at face value, you would discover that it isn't what it appears to be. What's really happening is that as soon as the child experiences frustration or failure—a Lego construction that falls apart or a toy that doesn't work properly—he's done. Or as soon as he even anticipates failure, he's through with that toy or that task and off to something new. When this pattern is repeated many times during a short period of time, e.g., five minutes, the picture is of an "inability" to focus and complete tasks. The behavior looks disorganized, spastic, impulsive.

When Debbie sees this pattern developing, she will bring the child back to the discarded item, often a Lego structure that didn't hold together, and will bring out a Lego helicopter kept specifically for such times. This helicopter has one pontoon that won't stay attached no matter what you do. Debbie gives the helicopter to the child and says, "Here, you can play with this." As soon as the child discovers that the pontoon won't stick, he's off to something new.

"Wait a second. Look at this," Debbie says as she tries unsuccessfully to make the pontoon stick to the underside of the helicopter. "Is it my fault that the pontoon won't stay on?" When the child agrees that the problem is with the faulty toy and not with the person trying to get it to stick together, Debbie brings the child back to the very first item he abandoned when he began to "impulsively" flit from thing to thing. "Give this another try," she says encouragingly. "I think you can make this work." Rare is the "ADD child" who doesn't return to Denis's office, where he and the child's parents are talking, much calmer, more focused, and much more optimistic. And this is during the first session.

Children do abandon toys or activities because they're genuinely not interested. Often, however, they move on because of the same frustrations and sense of failure that the children we work with experience in our playtherapy room. Children who feel like failures also typically feel like no one wants to spend time with them. This sets up a vicious cycle in which the child takes control of the anticipated rejection by distancing himself or by making himself eminently rejectable through his behavior.

If you gently bring your child back to the experience he has just fled— or bring the toy or game back to him—you can help him to complete whatever he was doing with a sense of accomplishment. Or demonstrate why the challenge was impossible in the first place. In either case, you will have intervened to break a pattern of giving up out of frustration while extending and refocusing your child's attention. Sometimes all it takes is a word of encouragement, while other times you may have to take a more active part in explaining or even fixing. When you repeat these positive patterns over time, you are literally shaping an attentional style at the very same time that you are helping to build your child's sense of accomplishment and self-esteem in the most natural of ways. This may seem like a little thing, especially given the multiple opportunities for failure or distraction presented by our overstimulated and overstimulating world, but it can be remarkably effective when done naturally and consistently over time. Adults intuitively slow down their movements and their speech when interacting with babies; they also both scale down and slow down their expectations. That same slowing down can be very useful with older children as well. When you intervene at moments of frustration to gently calm a child and give them a second chance at success, regardless of the activity, you decrease impulsiveness. All those other things we have mentioned that increase frustration tolerance and the ability to focus, concentrate, and get enjoyment out of an activity also contribute to slowing down impulsiveness.

Focus Attention by Acknowledging the Obvious

Just as with open secrets, failure to acknowledge the obvious promotes inattention, dissociative styles, and an overall "dumbing down" because the child cannot use all his faculties. One of the most common examples of this that we routinely encounter is when teachers arrange to meet privately with parents—usually mothers—so that they "won't talk about these things directly in front of the child." "These things" are invariably the child's behavior, clearly something the child already knows because the child has already experienced it. Adults, particularly mothers, tend to be very protective of children's feelings, often at the very same time they may be quite upset with them. This results in many things in children's lives never being straightforwardly acknowledged and thus never shared and dealt with. Not only does this communicate to the child that these things are much more serious than they need to be, it encourages the same kind of inattention and not-knowing that we find in more frankly dissociogenic situations. And it's unnecessary. You can still be supportive and understanding at the same time you acknowledge sad, unpleasant, or objectionable facts.

Get Rid of the Nintendo
But Keep the Computer

Some activities literally constitute training in dissociation and ADD behavior. So our advice is: Get rid of the stand-alone or hand-held electronic games as well as all the zap-'em-blow-'em-up games for the computer.

Computers are marvelous instruments. They can enrich experience and open up an extraordinary world of information and knowledge. As such, they are a marvelous *adjunct* to traditional learning. But they're not a replacement. For instance, learning how to read through books and being read to define learning and reading in terms of an *extended experience* that requires an effort to concentrate. It also defines them in terms of shared experience. Television, on the other hand, delivers a multisensorial experience without the slightest effort on the child's part, and computers are not far behind. Reading (or even listening to audio recordings) requires that the child engage in creative imagination. When there are no illustrations, the child must "fill in the blanks" for every aspect of the story. He has to imagine what the characters look like and how they relate to one another and to the environment. He has to give form and color to generically described objects such as the mountain, the airplane, the dragon. No such creative activity is required by the television or the computer. Even when the child has to provide input, answers, or solutions to educational computer programs, the experience is one of immediate reward and the nature of the "work" is very different.

Leave computers for the older child. Don't fall victim to the "computer literacy" craze and assume that the computer should be a key aspect of your child's daily experience and the learning process "from the very beginning," as is being advocated by some enthusiasts. Before you know it, the computer will have replaced *you*. When introduced too early or in the place of other experience, computers make for solitary experience, mesmerized absorption, and withdrawal from the world.

Take the time to create a solid foundation of experience, human relatedness, and the enterprising self-reliance that children knew forty or fifty years ago when they played together with whatever was at hand and didn't mind a bit of work to make their imaginations come alive. And listen to your child. The more you listen, the more you share his experience, the more your attention will prolong his attention. All of this will add to the openness and effectiveness of communication while facilitating healthy development.

9

Who's in Charge Here?

It's four o'clock and, as her son Frank gets home from school, Betty Rhoades is sitting in her living room having a cup of afternoon coffee with her good friend Janice Long.

"Hi, Mrs. Long," Frank says as he crosses the living room.

"Got any homework?" Betty asks.

"Nope, none today," Frank replies, slowing down momentarily on his way to the kitchen.

"I find that *hard* to believe," Betty stresses. Then, turning to look at her friend Janice at the other end of the couch, she says, "Report cards came home yesterday and *we* didn't do so well!" Betty raises her voice and turns toward the figure disappearing into the kitchen. "We *are* going to do better next time, *aren't* we, Frank?" A cursory "You bet, Mom" is heard as Frank heads out the back door with the soft drink he just grabbed from the fridge.

The Collective We and Individual Responsibility

Betty Rhoades is convinced that her son has a major problem. He won't take responsibility for anything—his room, his grades, his chores, the fights he gets into with his younger sister, nothing.

Later that evening, Betty will tell her husband that she had a word with Frank about his homework and his grades. But did she? Did Betty Rhoades really have a word with Frank about *his* homework and *his* grades? Not at all. By using "we" when she referred to her son and his efforts, the Collective We took responsibility for *his* grades, *his* homework, and *his* future performance. As soon as Frank heard his mother say that "report cards came home yesterday" and "*we* didn't do so well," Frank heard agency assigned and responsibility taken—by someone else. The interpersonal boundaries had been blurred. At the very best, "we" meant that responsibility was collectively shared—and everybody knows that it's always the other guy who gets to take the MOST responsibility.

In either case, Betty Rhoades just gave her son a brilliant, unconscious, easy way out. To avoid blurring these boundaries, parents should always use words and names that point directly to the individual—like "you," "me," "Jack," "them"—not collectives like "we" or "us."

DON'T	Take responsibility for someone else's actions or experience by saying "we."
	Use expressions like "Shall we take out the garbage" or "We didn't do well on our report card."
DO	Make it clear whom you are addressing or to whom you are referring. E.g., "Billy didn't do well on his report card" or "John, please take the garbage out now."

The Maternal Origin of the Collective We

At least part of the origin of this linguistic togetherness lies in the obligatory physical and emotional togetherness of mothering and child care. Newborns and infants are powerless to do anything for themselves and rely totally on the benevolence of adult care for everything, including their very survival. This means that much of what infants do is mediated by the caretaker, and the caretaker—at least traditionally in our society—has typically been the child's mother.

At the beginning of life, mothers are constantly helping their infant, applying a little support here, removing an obstacle there. Mothers are a kind of auxiliary self, an external facilitating self that, over the months and years, withdraws bit by bit from the developmental partnership to allow the child's individual identity and sense of personal autonomy and agency to develop.

It is impossible to know for sure (because we can't question infants about their experience), but it appears that children literally come to be *and literally grow into life* experiencing the "we-ness" of many of their developmental successes as if it were a part of them. And since Mother is constantly *doing for them*, her verbal descriptions that accompany this closeness also powerfully color the experience itself.

So, when an infant succeeds with Mother's help, who's responsible for the successful behavior? Infant? Mother? Or the Collective We?

It certainly makes sense that such intimate togetherness-in-action, combined with a constant blurring of interpersonal boundaries and identities, primes the developing child to be able to tune out—almost automatically—the conscious sense of personal agency and responsibility upon hearing "We . . ."

Be Nice to Mommy!

The first two and a half years of life allow for an immensely long and luxurious experience of togetherness. But as the child reaches the end of this stage, we routinely encourage parents to begin to use personal pronouns and names consistently when talking with their child. This helps focus attention and makes spoken language much clearer. Since there are lots of mommies and daddies in the world, using "I" and "me" to refer to yourself begins to make language much more specific. By two and a half children are extremely complex little beings, quite capable of understanding many of the nuances of language.

Using the personal pronouns "I" and "me" and possessives like "my" and "mine"—instead of "Mommy" and "Daddy" and "Mommy's" and "Daddy's"—makes what you're saying much more immediate, much more present.

Actually, it's these generic names "Mommy" and "Daddy" that depersonalize parents as children get older. Yet many mothers find it hard to make this transition. It feels to them as if they are distancing their child, putting an invisible language barrier between them. When these mothers complain that their children are aggressive or rude and disrespectful, we point out that it is much easier to be mean to a generic "Mommy" than it is to be mean to you. When a mother says, "Don't be mean to Mommy," whom is she referring to? It's up for grabs. But when a mother says, "Don't be mean to me!" the effect is immediate and the meaning is intensely localized. We think you'll find that transitioning from collective pronouns to specific personal pronouns around two and a half promotes autonomous behavior and responsibility while making aggression toward you just a bit harder for your toddler.

Since we've worked with many, many mothers who were still using the Collective We with older children, we've also had many opportunities to see how much longer it takes them to achieve the goals they set for their children's behavior and attitude than those mothers who make the transition quickly. Making the transition quickly doesn't mean that it will be painless, just that you will achieve what you actually want more quickly. If you feel a sense of disconnectedness when you transition from generic to personal pronouns, share your feelings and frustration with your spouse or with a friend. For your own peace of mind, however, remember that what you experience is not at all the same as what your child experiences. He or she is likely to feel the sense of distance that you may experience *only if you communicate that sense of discomfort and disconnectedness.* Remember too that your overall relationship with your child is the cumulative effect of everything you say and do. You can continue to build a solid and healthy relationship of trust and reliability even as you are changing your communication style.

Parental Communication Styles and Children's Responsibility

There are as many ways for parents to inadvertently sabotage their children's personal responsibility as there are ways for parents and children to interact. Like everything we have talked about so far, the complex process of throwing roadblocks in the path of children's responsibility is transparent. Rarely does anyone recognize when it's taking place.

Depersonalizing Children's Responsibility

Many adults totally depersonalize experience, behavior, and responsibility by using the nonspecific word "it." Again, a simple translation of Adultspeak tells us what adults really mean to say.

ADULTSPEAK	TRANSLATION
"It was an absolutely horrible week!"	"Jimmy was mean and disrespectful the entire week."
"It was a horrible birthday party!"	"Sally whined and complained throughout the entire party."
"It was one of the most embarrassing experiences I ever had!"	"Scott told his teacher to 'bug off' during the parent-teacher conference."

By using the totally impersonal "it" instead of saying "Sally or Billy did this or that," parents make it much easier for their children not to recognize themselves and their own actions in what is being described, making it infinitely easier for them to automatically dismiss whatever is being said because it is not about "them." In all three Adultspeak statements above, none of the words actually tell us who did what. The problem was the "bad week" or the "horrible time," not the child's behavior.

It may be that the more powerless parents feel to control or influence their children's behavior, the more painful it is to refer to it in highly personal form. Talking about "it" instead of being quite specific about what their own child said to the teacher may serve to soften the emotional blow or the personal embarrassment. Perhaps. But we think most people do it simply out of habit.

You can check this out for yourself just by comparing how young children and adults refer to both "good" and "bad" experiences. Adults tend to reduce a complex, extended experience—a trip or a vacation—to a single event by saying, "It was fantastic!" or "What a great trip!" Young children, on the other hand, tend to jump right into telling you about narrowly defined actual events ("I saw a mountain!" or "I fell off the boat!") without referring to the extended experience at all.

So, be specific—de-rrify your language if you want children to really hear what you're trying to say. Remember, too, that when children hear that "the whole week was a disaster" or "was ruined," they know they can't possibly turn it around—certainly not a "whole week." This removes realistic incentives to do anything differently at this point. Besides, it's not *their* fault. It's the week's fault. . . .

DON'T	Diffuse responsibility for someone else's actions by referring to them as "it." E.g., "It was a mess!"
DO	Make it clear whom you are addressing or to whom you are referring. E.g., "Billy trashed his room," "Sally got an A in math."

Discrediting Elective Behavior

Parents desperately want their children to behave responsibly. They want their children to do what's expected of them and to follow directions—to do what they're told. Parents also want their children to accept responsibility. And yet parents routinely discredit the very responsible elective behavior they desire through off-handed explanations. If Fred has routinely slacked off on his homework but this week managed to finish it all on time, do Fred's parents give him the 100 percent credit he both needs and deserves? Not typically. Instead, we hear a trailer at the end of the positive statement: "But we set a timer. . . ." The qualifier gives the timer the credit, not Fred. And the implied message is that, without the timer, there is no way in the world that Fred would ever have completed his homework.

Sally got up, got dressed, ate her breakfast, and made it to school without a single fuss, without the teacher ever having to send a note home. So does Sally get the 100 percent credit that she both needs and deserves? Hardly! Instead, we hear "But it was only a three-day week."

Another very common disclaimer is "But we gave her warnings." Whatever the child has done is immediately discredited because it was done "under duress."

Give 100 Percent Credit for Even Reluctant Compliance

In therapy, if a child does the right thing—whatever it may be—Debbie gives him or her 100 percent credit. And with great fanfare. The child gets 100 percent credit even if what was done was done by accident. *After just a few such experiences, the behavior genuinely belongs to the child.* If you want desired behavior to become "real," never discredit it by explaining, justifying, or minimizing it.

Even if the behavior you get reeks of fakeness, accept it fully and give the child every bit of positive reinforcement you can. We have worked with many children or adolescents over the years whose behavior and attitudes were so repugnant that no one even wanted to get close to them, let alone become enthusiastic in their presence, yet Debbie always gives these children every ounce of credit she can muster. In return, they often end up doing for her what they had never done before for adults who they knew disliked and distrusted them. Even with such children, the results can be real, meaningful, and enduring. Besides, your only alternative is to be the unpaid engineer of a very negative self-fulfilling prophecy.

Setting Yourself Up to Be Proved Wrong

We were in the Washington, D.C., Metro a few years ago when a tourist family of four boarded our train. The mother, father, and eight- or nine-year-old sister continued on past us, settling on the opposite side at the very end of the car. The twelve- or thirteen-year-old son stopped right in the middle of the aisle about ten feet from them. Unlike the other three members of his preppy family, the son was in full skateboard-hip-hop regalia, right down to the baggy pants, two sets of visible underwear, a skater haircut, and a backward baseball cap.

"Come on over here," the father said, patting the space he had saved for his son. When his son made no sign of doing what he was told, the father said, a bit more forcefully, "Jack, come over here and sit down." Jack shook his head no, frowned, but said nothing. "JACK," the father said, now much more forcefully, "we're heading for a big turn. At least hold on to the pole. You're going to fall down!"

Then the dad watched with frustrated embarrassment as Jack spread his legs for better balance, then swayed gracefully as the cars jerked from side to side. The train rounded the curve at full speed, but Jack looked like a surfer deftly riding an undulating wave. The train straightened out and came to a rather abrupt halt, causing the mother and sister to slide into the father, squeezing him up against the end of the car and aggravating him even more. Jack, who had negotiated the abrupt stop as gracefully as he had ridden out the rocky turn, bent to a gunslinger's pose. With his two thumbs up and pointing his index fingers at his father, Jack held his hands out as if they were guns.

"Psych, dude!" Jack said to his father, drawing out each word with the kind of swagger that is the specialty of insolent adolescents. "You was dead w-r-o-n-g!"

Don't Set Yourself Up

The D.C. Metro scenario is a trap that many parents inadvertently set for themselves *by unnecessarily giving explanations as justification for what would have otherwise been a straightforward command.* When whatever was described or predicted by the parent doesn't happen, the child has proved the parent wrong, thereby destroying the parent's authority.

DON'T	Treat children as if they are owed an explanation or justification for your every rule or decision.
	Feel that you are an ogre when you say, "Because I said so" if what you are doing is in your children's best interest.

DO	Make your parental decisions based on your children's needs for safety, security, stability, etc.
	Provide structure and values by exercising genuine benevolent parental authority.
	ISSUE COMMANDS, e.g., "Come sit with us," "Please clean up your room."

Once again, expressions like "You need to . . ." or "If you don't, then . . ." carry a Double Whammy. They give the child's logical mind the opportunity to dismiss what should be a command with the automatic response "No, I don't!" When a child who has been told that she will get hit by a car if she plays in the street, plays in the street and doesn't get hit, she has proven that it's "safe" to play in the street. And she has the force of absolutely impeccable logic on her side. Giving a specific reason simply sets the parent up to be proved wrong by experience.

We're Not Really Banning Explanations

We're not saying that parents should never explain to children the dangers of certain things such as playing in the street or touching the stove. Of course they should. But many parents confuse providing a justification for why the child should follow their directions with the directions themselves. Parental explanations are designed to further the growth of understanding, an ongoing process that lasts years. Commands are instantaneous: when you issue a command, you want results NOW, plain and simple.

When you want results NOW, you can increase your communication effectiveness, and improve your child's behavioral compliance as well, by not adding justifications and explanations. There will be time later, when safety or expediency are not the pressing issues, to do the appropriate explaining or educating.

Asking a Child If It's Okay to Be a Parent

Many people have quirks in their spoken language. These are personal speaking styles in which basically normal speech patterns are peppered with particular words or phrases such as "Right?" or "Know what I mean?" Many parents have the habit of ending many of their sentences with "okay?" Often this is nothing more than a habit. But for some parents, it may be an attempt to soften what they perceive to be the harshness of a straightforward command. In either case, ending your sentences with "okay?" puts you in the spot of asking your child's permission to say whatever it is that you've just said.

We had one particular experience that illustrated just how subtle but powerful such inadvertent permission-asking can be. Jerry, a minuscule four-year-old boy, had disclosed to us that he had been sexually abused by his father, a man who was known to be extremely aggressive and violently vindictive. Because this little boy's father's violent behavior was so scary, even to adults, everyone involved with Jerry prior to the notification of law enforcement was quite concerned about whether the boy would talk freely with an officer.

The Crimes Against Children officer was an attractive young woman in her early thirties. Warm, pleasant, and very child-friendly, she leaned over so as to be at Jerry's level. There was really nothing about this young woman that one couldn't like, all of which contributed to an atmosphere, one would think, that should have made Jerry comfortable enough to trust this kind "police lady."

As a sign of her authority, and to make the four-year-old feel safe enough to talk openly with her, she began the interview by introducing herself and producing her gun, her shiny badge, and her photo I.D. Then Officer Brown leaned even closer, raised her eyebrows like adults do when talking to very young children, and asked, "Is it okay if I ask you a few questions?" The four-year-old's eyes darted back and forth, a look of confusion on his face. Finally, he nodded okay.

"Can you tell me your last name?" We looked at one another and winced. We knew what Officer Brown was trying to do—determine whether the child would be a credible witness—but we also knew she had just doomed the whole exercise.

Jerry hesitated, his eyes still darting around the room. Finally, he shook his head no. Officer Brown continued.

"Do you know when your birthday is?" We both shuddered as Jerry once again shook his head no. Officer Brown paused briefly, then continued with her questions.

"Do you know what the difference is between the truth and a lie?" Jerry looked even more confused and just stared at Officer Brown.

"Can I ask you a question and see?" she asked, again raising her eyebrows to indicate her anticipation of a positive answer. Jerry nodded yes.

"Do you know your mom's name?" Jerry blinked and nodded yes.

"Is your mom's name Sally?" Jerry shook his head no and laughed, at last breaking the ice.

"Is it Jean?" Officer Brown asked.

"No!" Jerry said. "It's Betty!"

Despite her genuine attempts to be child-friendly, Officer Brown's use of questions instead of commands, her invitation of negative responses, and her repetitive suggestions that Jerry might not be able to answer her questions could serve as a negative "self-test and review" for all the lessons of this book. Her worst offense, though, was that this absolute paragon of authority began her encounter with a child by surrendering that very authority. After producing the symbols of her power—her I.D., her badge, and her gun—kindly Officer Brown asked a very small and terrified child for permission to ask him questions. We can imagine what must have gone through Jerry's mind. *If this lady with the badge and the gun has to get **my** permission just to ask me questions, she's no match for my crazy dad. She can't possibly protect me! He'll trash us both!*

Ultimately, Officer Brown concluded that four-year-old Jerry could not be formally qualified as a credible witness, but the tongue-tied space-case triggered by her inept questioning was simply not the same child we saw regularly in our office. The Jerry we knew was bright and very articulate. Luckily, his safety did not depend upon his ability to testify. Jerry's father confessed as soon as he learned that law enforcement was involved and ended up spending fifteen months in prison.

Power and Empowerment

Many therapists reason correctly that bad experiences, and trauma particularly, take away a child's sense of agency, control, and mastery, so they set about trying to reinstate all three. But they go about it in entirely the wrong manner—they essentially relinquish control of the process of therapy to the child. They allow the child to take the initiative, to choose the materials, and to shape the direction of the interaction of the therapy, believing that children's play is itself curative and all adults have to do is to set the stage for the "healing power of play."

Some child therapists, like some parents, tend to see empowerment in terms of a *distribution of power*. Since the hurt, traumatized, or abused child has been on the losing end of the power distribution, therapy has to right the imbalance. Hurt children are seen as "needing" this kind of power, and so they are allowed or encouraged to beat up the abusive parent doll or to control the process of therapy. Even nonabused and nontraumatized children with poor self-esteem are allowed to "win" at games of skill against a clearly superior adult player, as if this could somehow right that balance of power and control.

"If he's doing this all the time, he must really *need* to!" many mothers have said to us over the years. But these indulged children don't get better. They don't become kinder, gentler, nor does their behavior or academic and interpersonal performance generally improve. And these children certainly don't experience an increase in genuine self-esteem. They just become bigger, more controlling powermongers.

The Omnipotent Powerless Child Syndrome

Many of the children we work with—many of whom have *not* been abused or traumatized—have the world wrapped around their little finger. This is what we call the "omnipotent powerless child syndrome." These children hurt. They break and destroy. They manipulate. They terrorize. They don't follow any rules. They have immense power, yet these children do not have the "power" simply to be liked for who they are. These children have the power to wreak havoc in the world of adults, *but they can't even make a friend.*

Real Power Versus Pushing Parents' Buttons

Genuine empowerment comes from simple successes and freedoms, not from the ability to hurt back.

When Dad lives in another town (perhaps with another mom and other children), doesn't pay child support, forgets the child's birthday, Christmas or Hanukkah, and other holidays, and promises to come or call and doesn't, is there anything the child can do to change him? No. Such children are truly powerless.

Normally, we all have the subjective power to "control" other people. Say something and they respond. Make good grades and they give you praise. Smile and they smile back. Under "normal" circumstances, our very existence "makes" other people pay attention to us and to care. All we have to do is just be ourselves. This power is so elemental, so subtle that rarely are we consciously aware of it. The child with a disconnected nonresponsive parent has lost this elemental power to elicit love, care, respect, attention, and even basic interest. Under such circumstances, there is absolutely nothing—from the best behavior to the best grades—that the child can do to elicit the positive behavioral responses he craves.

In the midst of this sense of powerlessness, some children discover—simply in the course of everyday life—that they have another power, the power to push adults' buttons. Almost without trying, you can make big adults behave in absolutely predictable ways. You can elicit anger, rage, frustration, yelling, and screaming. Granted, there's a price to pay for all this subtle power: getting in trouble, losing privileges, getting grounded, etc. But at least it works. And it's *very* reliable. In fact, this kind of power is magic. It's *action at a distance*. All it takes to get a grown adult to behave in perfectly predictable fashion—all the way across the room!—is the appropriate little gesture at the appropriate time. Now that's power! And that's control!

Children Really Do Want Adults to Be in Charge

And power is addictive. Children, even very young children, love the feeling. They'll take every ounce they can get.

And yet, deep down inside, children don't really want all that power. Deep down inside, children know that they can't manage the world. Without the benevolent care and authority of adults, children couldn't survive. Deep down inside, even the most power-hungry little terrorizing Masters of the Universe know that the more power they get, the less stable and the more threatening the world becomes. The illusory antidote to this loss of control over the real world is to get more, more, MORE power—even in the face of their deep-down inner knowledge that the more they disempower adults the more vulnerable they are.

Disempowering Little Button-Pushers

If you find yourself caught up in your child's exhausting button-pushing behavior, there may be a surprisingly easy way to bring it to an end. *Just don't react.* Easier said than done, of course, but often that's all it takes—plus patience and consistency. When your child can no longer push your negative buttons, he or she will eventually have to switch to the positive ones. It's a process of attrition. In any case, you know that the power struggles that ensue when you react to having your buttons pushed lead nowhere, so that's reason enough to opt out of that behavior. (Even though it may feel, at first, like you're allowing your child to "win.")

Real Power

Knowing that one can play house, play cars, or play ball with one's friends without worrying about being hurt is a form of empowerment when one is five years old. Not having to worry about whether other children will "see right through you" and think you are "filthy and disgusting" is a form of empowerment when you are ten and have been sexually abused. Knowing that you can count on the consistency, continuity, and predictability of a benevolent adult world is a form of empowerment when you are seven and have been told both to follow and to break rules by the same adult who abused and terrified you. Being able to finish your schoolwork—and even get a good grade—when before you couldn't even concentrate long enough to get more than a D or an F: *that* is empowerment in the life of a child. Knowing that you can get adults to like you without hurting, exploiting, or abusing you: *that* is empowerment in the life of a child. Being able to sleep soundly at night in a safe place without worrying about whether *these* adults will sneak in in the middle of the night and force you into oral sex: *that* is empowerment in the life of an abused or traumatized child. Not feeling that you're always wrong: *that* is empowerment in the life of a child who has been treated as "stupid," "disgusting," and "retarded" by a parent who didn't really care.

The Perils of Family Democracy

Stevie Jones is a seven-year-old second grader about to get himself suspended for the third time in as many weeks.

"Sit down, put your hand up, and wait your turn just like everyone else!" his teacher yells, sick and tired of dealing with this in-your-face oppositional, defiant, and disrespectful child.

"Why should I!" Stevie launches back. He shakes his head with a look that says "You're wasting my time."

Little Stevie Jones has racked up quite a list of "charges" from school personnel: talking out of turn, interrupting and failing to complete classroom work, forgetting homework or simply not bothering to turn it in, refusing to remain seated on the school bus, refusing to follow hall rules.

And he's not exactly a constant source of joy at home, either. He treats his mother exactly the same way. He won't do chores or clean up his room. While he's very rude and disrespectful toward his mom and dad, it hasn't yet stopped him from expecting them to respond to his desires as if he had always been the kindest and most respectful of children for whom it's such a delight to do things. It is very hard to get Stevie to take part in family activities or, for that matter, just to tear him away from his TV or computer games. Exasperated when all the in-house solutions fail, the school suggests that Stevie and his parents see a counselor.

In counseling, Stevie's mom is asked to explain the laissez-faire approach she and her husband have taken to their only child.

"My parents raised me like dictators," she begins. "They never explained anything to me. They never told me why I should do this or that. I just had to do it, that's all. Say 'Yes, ma'am,' 'Yes, sir,' and do it. You would have thought I was in the army, not in a family. When I was a child, I promised myself that if I ever had kids, I would treat them with respect. I would tell them why I was telling them to do this or that, why they had to follow rules, and what those rules were for. I didn't want any child of mine to have to live through what I lived through. Children have rights, just as much as adults. They should be treated like they had a brain and weren't just some robot that had to take orders mindlessly. I wanted my children to question authority, not to be crushed by it like I was."

Most of the time parents aren't this aware of just how much they're making up for their own past experiences when they work so hard to provide alternatives for their own children. The home in which Mrs. Jones grew up was not a genuinely benevolent home; it was an intolerant and autocratic home. In a *genuinely* benevolent home, do children really need to have explicit rights? No, all they really require is to have their physical and emotional needs met.

Out of the best of intentions, Mrs. Jones had equipped her son with what she had needed as a child to maintain her sense of indivi-

duality, autonomy, and self-worth. But since Mrs. Jones had never been insensitive or autocratic, she had had no reason to equip her son with the psychological armor necessary to withstand the onslaught of her dictatorial parents. In fact, Mrs. Jones was an entirely different sort of person, a kind, perceptive, and gentle person, attuned to others. She just needed to believe more in herself and to realize that no sales job was required for her to convey to her son her very real respect and affection.

Benevolent Parental Authority

What's a parent? *A parent is a big person who tells a little person what to do— for the right reasons and because they genuinely care.* If you're not insensitive, demeaning, or abusive, if you don't lack all good judgment and common sense, it's simply not necessary to justify or explain. Developing children don't need explanations for benevolent authority. But they do need structure, rules, and boundaries that caring parents can create and maintain with consistency and continuity over time. Benevolent parental authority doesn't crush children. On the contrary, it helps to assure the safety and security that children need in order to grow and learn. Love, care, and respect are not to be found in words but only in actions and relationships. Genuinely benevolent authority conveys your care and your respect for your child's needs.

Many parents don't seem to realize that, like it or not, they really are in charge. They try to escape this realization by pretending that they're not really providing the basic values, that they're not really shaping their child's mind, behavior, tastes, and styles. They pretend that they can somehow delegate some of this responsibility directly to the child by introducing "freedom" early in their child's life. But while you aren't the only formative factor in your child's life, you do have immense power to shape it. If you believe in your own values, and if you're willing to learn from experience and change when necessary, then don't worry about the responsibility. Accept it. Welcome it. And make the very best of it.

"But I Really Do Want My Child to Question Authority!"

Everyone questions authority in this country, and the result tends to be chaos and shoot-from-the-hip opinionism. Children are constantly saying, "But I've got the right to my own opinion!" This lovely right turns out, much of the time, to be *the right to be just as mistaken, opinionated, or wrong-headed as the next guy*! Oddly enough, the more some children question authority, the less they tend to think for themselves.

The keyword in the expression "question authority" is not *authority* but *question*. To really question authority means to be able to ask such good questions that authority will actually have to think in order to respond. If you want your child to really learn how to question authority, don't tell him that he, like everyone, has a right to his own opinion. Instead, be a benevolent authority and tell your child what to do and when to do it. Put structure, rules, and boundaries into your child's experiential world from the very beginning of his or her life. If you do, then later, much later—at seven or eight—when your child says to you, "Mom (or Dad), I think you're wrong," your child won't be exercising bogus dead-end rights or shooting wildly from the hip. He or she will be able to tell you *why* they think you're wrong. It's not necessary to force independent thinking. Just cultivate *good* thinking. And make sure that you provide the reliable environmental structure and values within which good thinking can flourish.

How to Raise a Successful Revolutionary

Some parents want their children to do more than just question authority. They want them to change the world. "Won't all those years of telling my child what to do kill that possibility?" they ask. Absolutely not! You can't change the world if you don't know how to successfully structure your own experience, your own thoughts, and your own behavior. Children just don't know enough to be revolutionaries in their own time. They have to grow up. They have to learn and acquire knowledge, perspective, and judgment. And they have to think clearly and creatively enough to be able to recognize a revolutionary thought when they have one or encounter one. Unless you want that to happen solely by chance, don't try to micromanage independence. Don't read children their rights prematurely. Just be a benevolent parental authority in your child's life.

10

"Choose to Be
Your Real, Terrific, Good Self!":
Agency, Freedom, and
Responsibility for Tots

Over the years, Debbie has asked many children in therapy, "Are babies born good or bad?" It's amazing how many children reply, "Bad." Many of these children believe that they themselves were born bad. Some believe that other children were born bad and that you can tell this by their bad behavior. It's not hard to tell where these ideas came from in children who were taught the doctrine of Original Sin. But many of the children who believed themselves to have been "born bad" had never had such religious indoctrination. They also had parents who had made a very conscious effort to distinguish the act from the child. These parents were convinced that their children's sense of being "bad" couldn't be due to hearing themselves called "bad." Somehow, these children had developed a very negative self-image.

We had also found that when we asked parents to tell us, at the beginning of the session, about their child's behavior during the interval since our last meeting, they would always begin with negative and objectionable behavior. Even if the child had been perfectly behaved for the entire week since our last session, the first—and perhaps only—thing we would hear about was the tantrum the child threw in the car on the way to our office. We also noticed that when we asked them why their child had behaved badly, parents would often reply that the child "did it for attention."

To help parents remember the events of the week, and to help them differentiate between "bad" and "sad" (a crucial distinction that we'll talk more about in chapter 11), we devised what we called a "Smiley Chart," a half-piece of plain typing paper with the days of the week divided into morning and afternoon-evening. The parent's job was to put a big Smiley (or Sad) Face or a little "Grrr" or "Growlie," depending upon the child's behavior. A tantrum, physical aggression, or destructiveness would obviously get a "Grrr," while good behavior would get a Smiley, and appropriate sadness, a sad face. To make sure that both good behavior and genuine sadness got the positive attention they both deserved, we had the parents make the happy and sad faces big and in color and the "Grrr"s small and in pencil.

On the lower right-hand side of the paper, we wrote three simple sentences that sum up the solution to many childhood problems:

> Be your real, terrific, good self!
> Follow directions first time!
> No mean stuff!

Our unassuming little tool helped both parents and children distinguish clearly between bad and sad behavior, and it certainly forced parents to record and acknowledge their children's good behavior, which otherwise often went unnoticed and unacknowledged. We were fairly happy with it for several years. Until we met Bobby.

Learning About Freedom and Choice from Little Kids

Bobby was a seven-year-old blind, retarded child who was a great source of frustration for his parents and his teacher. His teacher was frustrated because she couldn't proceed to the next step in his training—learning how to walk with a cane—because Bobby steadfastly refused to engage in the prerequisite behavior—finding his way around with his extended arms as a buffer. Instead, he just smashed into things, especially when the surroundings were unfamiliar. (In his own space, Bobby could navigate quite well. He could, for example, spend hours riding his two-wheel bike round and round on the family driveway without ever falling down or going over the edge.) But given Bobby's refusal to use his extended arms as cane equivalents, his teacher was stymied.

For his parents, Bobby was a source of joy simply because he existed. He had weighed barely more than a pound and a half at birth and survival had been a struggle. But Bobby not only survived his infancy, he seemed to be quite intense and quite stubborn about getting on with life. Unfortunately, he was also stubborn about other things as well.

It didn't take long for us to realize why Bobby refused to use his arms to find his way around. It wasn't just stubbornness. It was his belief that it wasn't really necessary. After all, if his very survival was a miracle, as his family—impassioned charismatic Catholics—believed it was, then it was only a matter of time until God worked another miracle and gave him sight.

As soon as Bobby's reasoning became clear, we said, "Bobby, God has given you everything that He is going to give you. Instead of you waiting around for God to give you sight, God is waiting for you to get off your rear end and put your arms out so that you can learn to use a cane!" With that, Bobby did.

From Being to Choosing

Even though Bobby was blind, Debbie made up a chart for him, just as she would for any of the children we work with. Bobby couldn't see the chart, but he could *feel* it. So Debbie bought the kind of foam weather-stripping that's used to insulate doors and a few self-adhesive sanding disks. The soft weatherstripping became Bobby's Smileys and the rough self-adhesive sandpaper, cut into small circles, became his "Grrr"s.

To our surprise, Bobby's behavior quickly worsened, but we soon realized that Bobby absolutely *loved* the feel of the rough sandpaper—so we simply dropped it and just left the place blank that would have been occupied by a "Grrr."

The week after we explained to Bobby that God was waiting for him to use the good arms that He had given him, Bobby's mother was absolutely delighted with her son's behavior. She had only one complaint. On Sunday morning, as he traditionally did every Sunday, Bobby climbed

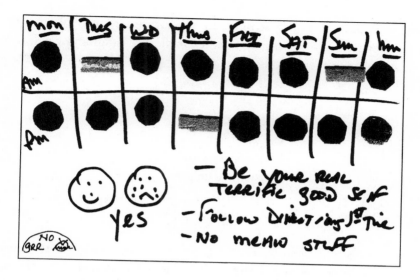

into bed with his parents. This time, however, he crawled up on top of his dad, turned around, and farted right in his dad's face.

"Bobby!" we said. "Why did you do that?"

"Because I CHOSE to," Bobby said with a beatific smile on his face.

Are Children Agents or Objects?

Although no one was happy with what Bobby did, everyone was delighted that, for the very first time in his life, Bobby admitted that he CHOSE to do it. From that day on, well over ten years prior to the writing of this book, we changed the first sentence on our little chart to read: **Choose** to be your real, terrific, good self!

Denis keeps Bobby's old Smiley Chart in the bookcase beside his chair. When a parent protests that he "lost it" or that he can't control himself, Denis takes out the chart, shows it to the parent, and says, "Here's a Smiley Chart for a blind, retarded seven-year-old. He can't even see it. He's got to feel it. Yet it still says **Choose** to be your real, terrific, good self! So, if we can reasonably expect a blind, retarded seven-year-old to choose to be his real, terrific, good self, then we can certainly expect it of an adult!" This usually gets our message across.

The fact is, language is full of expressions that deny our basic freedom.

Responsibility is routinely attributed to everything from a sibling or the weather or fatigue to, occasionally, the Devil. Just listen and you'll hear such expressions everywhere:

- But she hit me!
- I had to.
- It was too hard.
- It's not my fault.
- I couldn't help it.
- I was tired.
- My brain made me.

These expressions are very much like those used by parents to depersonalize or diffuse personal responsibility that we discussed in the last chapter, except that these things are said by children. Even very young children routinely speak (and obviously reason) as if circumstances dictate much of their behavior, as if outside forces make them do what they do. (Occasionally they even treat "inside" sources as if they were "outside," as when the child says, "My brain made me.") When both parents and children are using a vocabulary like that to describe otherwise elective behavior, clearly it's not very reasonable to expect anyone really to be in control.

Choose to Be Your Real, Terrific, Good Self!

From the very first encounter, we expect even very young children—three- and four-year-olds—to change their own behavior. When three-and-a-half-year-old Mary tells her mom that her brother knocked over her dollhouse, instead of hurting him back or breaking something of his, her mom says, "What a good choice! I am so proud of you for coming to tell me, and not being mean back."

Occasionally, Debbie will say to a child in the parents' presence, "Do Denis and I go home with you? Do we go to school with you? No! So who made all those good choices?" "I did!" says the child—even boys up to ten or so—and they light up like a Christmas tree. With the exception of occasionally giving the child the opportunity to take credit for his good choices in front of his parents, we allow the choice to remain implicit in the child's behavior, in his or her actions. We don't drill children on agency and choice and we certainly don't engage in philosophical discussions. We just give the child 100 percent credit for the good things he or she does, and we do so very clearly in terms of choice.

Immediately after Bobby's announcement that he had *chosen* to do what he did, we changed the way we begin each session. Instead of asking the parents how the child's *week* was, we say, "Tell us about his good choices since we saw you last." Not infrequently parents will say that there weren't any, but we never accept that massively negative characterization of the child's behavior over a period as long as a week. "Sure there were," we say. "There had to be some. Tell us about them." We point out to the parents we work with that, even if their child ended up in "jail for kids"—the juvenile detention center—we would still start the session with a review of the good choices.

This sounds naïve and idealistic, to be sure, but it's really only a consistent message to the child that they are capable of choice and that our consistent expectations are that they will make good choices.

Watch the Conventional Language!

As usual, conventional language and everyday expressions can sabotage your best efforts. If you want to stress your child's ability to choose, do not use expressions like "What kind of boy were you today?" or "Were you a good girl today?" If your child was "bad" that day, then that's the explanation of their behavior. Don't expect your child to behave responsibly if he or she is bad. The phrase suggests that it's part of their nature.

Children commonly say things like "If I'm good today, can I . . . ?" or "If I'm good, will you . . . ?" Listen carefully for expressions like these and correct them on the spot. A bad choice can be changed, but if a child is "bad," then the badness is part of the child's identity and can't change. Children who view themselves, rather than their choices, as bad often think their parents would like to get rid of *them*. These kids will frequently save their parents the trouble by "getting rid" of themselves by staying disconnected and separate.

Over time, these things take their toll. It makes no sense to attribute an "inappropriately negative self-image" or the "bad" noncompliant behavior to formal psychiatric disorders like depression or oppositional-defiant disorder when the language of parents and children alike routinely refers to the child as "bad."

Undoing Negative Self-Images with Good Choices

Let's say you have an eight-year-old who is a royal pain. He's oppositional, defiant, mean, nasty, and doesn't have many friends because he seems to preempt any possibility of rejection by being off-putting from the very first encounter with a new classmate or playmate. He's never really happy, but he's also rarely sad in the normal, healthy sense of the term. Can you turn that around with choice? Sure. In fact, everyday life will give you many opportunities to do so.

Let's say that the two of you are playing chess or checkers. Initially, your child is impulsive because he wants to win. But he wants to win because he really doesn't want to lose. Losing is another sign that he's bad and stupid. Just play along calmly until your child makes a wise move, then say something like, "Oh, I really like it when you choose to protect yourself! Good going!" The next time he does the same, say, "Great choice!" As you intermittently emphasize choice and being self-protective, you will very subtly redefine your child's notion of being in charge. Being in charge will change—sometimes very quickly and, other times, more slowly—into *enjoying the game and making it last longer*. As the games become longer, you can comment on how much more fun it is just to keep the game going than to rush to win. Of course, making a game like checkers or chess last longer means making the relationship last longer. The longer you play enjoyably with someone, the more comfortably connected you feel. So, with something as simple as a common board game, you can (1) define spontaneously occurring adaptive behavior in terms of choice; (2) redefine the child's self in terms of something worth protecting; (3) decrease impulsiveness; and (4) improve relationships.

Don't wait and wait until the child does something major. What makes tactics such as this effective is that opportunities for using them occur frequently, often in the middle of otherwise negative behavior. We have found that it is the very rare child who doesn't respond to such mundane positive communications, even if they began as the nastiest, most off-putting kid you ever met.

Follow Directions First Time!

The work environment of preschool teachers is much more like the average home than like the average elementary school classroom. Preschool teachers and daycare providers who have used our methods have found that they can significantly decrease disruptive and aggressive behaviors while promoting an overall sense of cooperation in their environment.

When a preschool teacher praises a child's compliance with, "I really like it when you follow directions the first time!" she is telling the child something very positive about him- or herself as well as about her expectations and their relationship. When she adds, "I really like it when you *choose* to follow directions the first time!" she is communicating her belief in the child as a free agent, as someone not only capable of making choices but of making good choices.

Notice that no teaching or lecturing is required. Young children don't need to have lessons on good and bad choices. All they need is for an adult to recognize their good choices in the course of everyday activities and to be given full credit for them.

Notice also that there is no stress on bad choices. Even very young children understand what a bad choice is, especially when adults structure communication and experience so that making good choices is routinely recognized and acknowledged. Even very young children will begin to define as "bad choices" whatever behaviors fall outside the range of behaviors that they experience as affirming and enhancing on a regular basis. That's how to communicate values and how to help children quickly change bad choices, not with long talks about what's right and what's wrong.

No Mean Stuff!

When the everyday emphasis is on a communication style that highlights compliance, cooperation, sharing, and using adult resources—even in the midst of really objectionable child behavior—the need to focus on negative behavior will begin to decrease. Even when a child does something unacceptable, like hitting back, breaking something, or not sharing, you must provide a consequence (see below) but then say something like "I bet you'll come and tell me next time instead of hitting." By creating a context of positive communication and positive expectations, when you occasionally need to tell a child directly what not to do, the effect is much greater. By doing so, you also provide your child many opportunities throughout the day to make and enjoy good choices.

Consequences, Not Punishment

If the goal is to raise a child who recognizes choice, makes the right choice most of the time, and who takes responsibility for his actions, then discipline should facilitate the process, not interfere with it. Unfortunately, most punishment hurts children, which only teaches the child to hurt others in turn. Punishment keeps up the cycle of revenge and, by example, gives the child permission to be mean—the exact opposite of what you are trying to communicate to your child. And in general, most punishment requires that the child admit in one form or another that he or she is bad.

Time-Outs

With infants, no discipline whatsoever is needed. Just say no and redirect the child. Most parents begin to discipline as such with toddlers, an implicit recognition that their child has arrived at an age when choice is finally meaningful. It's at this time that parents begin to punish and to use disciplinary interventions.

The time-out does just what its name implies: it takes the child out of the social context for a particular length of time. Parents put children in corners, so-called time-out chairs, or send them to their rooms. (Don't use a child's bedroom for discipline or punishment and then expect them to enjoy playing or sleeping there.) Some parents (and teachers and daycare providers) tell children to "think about it" while in time-out. Rarely do these interventions work.

There are all sorts of technical variations on the time-out that lack even common sense but have a "developmental" sound to them. One of the most common is matching the length of the time-out in minutes to the child's age in years. According to this formula, a six-year-old would be given a six-minute time-out. Not only do such formulas lack any real developmental foundation, they make it too easy for parents and early childhood professionals to fail to think about what such interventions are supposed to accomplish and whether they actually work.

Young children learn by doing and experiencing, not through lectures or forced meditation, so *the purpose of a time-out is (1) to stop a behavior that is deemed unacceptable and (2) to reintegrate the child as quickly as possible back into the positive activity that was interrupted by the child's unacceptable behavior.* A successful time-out reinstitutes acceptable behavior as quickly as possible—instantaneously in some cases. Most time-outs fail because they are too long, too complicated, and actually invite the child to perpetuate a power struggle with the supervising adult. All the child has to do to pull the adult back into an active power struggle is to say no or stick out his tongue.

Successful time-outs with young children have a very simple structure: Interrupt the objectionable activity by grasping the child's arms *gently but firmly* while saying, "That's a time-out. No [hitting, biting, screaming, whatever]." Then count, "One, two, three, four, five," and say, "Time-out's over." Do this in a very matter-of-fact tone. With the end of the time-out, turn the child gently back toward whatever he or she was doing before the time-out. If you're involved in the activity that was interrupted by the child's unacceptable behavior, simply resume it as if nothing happened. If you're not, just let the child pick up where he or she was before the time-out was necessary.

If the child appears to resist the time-out immediately (i.e., moves immediately as you begin the time-out), simply declare, "Time-out's over" immediately and repeat the process as necessary. The child will become confused shortly as to who is actually controlling the time-out and will come to accept the intervention. This avoids all confrontation and power struggles entirely while providing an implicit consequence and also permitting the child to move on.

Some children respond immediately to time-outs while others require many time-outs over a short period of time. In fact, when appropriate, we use time-outs during the first playtherapy encounter to see how well a young child responds to adult interventions and benevolent structure and also as an instantaneous intervention for any self-harm, as when a child hits himself in the head because he messed up on a Lego creation. Notice that here, too, the purpose is to communicate our values and our expectations: not even a child who thinks he's bad and awful deserves to be hit. Parents and therapists who intervene by asking a child, "Why did you do that?" don't realize that they never stopped the process, never said that the behavior is unacceptable, and never said "Don't do it!" All of that is communicated simultaneously by the brief and instantaneous time-out.

It's important to keep in mind that "many time-outs" really does mean many time-outs. As in any experiential intervention with children, some children are quick responders and some have extremely resistant behavioral styles. So don't give up if you don't get instant results. Your potential effectiveness lies in the consistency, continuity, and predictability of your interventions, not in intensity or your child's conscious awareness of the process. All you want to do is stop the objectionable behavior, thereby creating an alternative positive behavior pattern. When used together with matter-of-fact but unequivocal communication about the child's inherent goodness, such simple interventions can work extremely well.

Consequences for Choices

Because it can convey a sense of vindictiveness or retribution, most *punishment* allows even adolescents to have a "You're being mean!" reaction. As we've already said, this completely changes the subject from whatever the child or adolescent has done or failed to do to focus on your behavior as a parent. If you want children or adolescents to make the connection between their choices and the consequences that ensue, let the consequences do the convincing. This requires emotional neutrality and a matter-of-fact attitude on your part. No lectures, forced confessions, or meditations on the meaning of one's behavior are required. (When the police officer hands you a speeding ticket, he doesn't then tell you to pull over and spend fifteen minutes "thinking about what you've just done." The consequence is the fine, the points on your license, and an increase in your insurance premium. If the officer does try to rub it in, you're much more likely to drive off paying more attention to your anger than to your driving, in which case you haven't learned a thing.) So don't invite a self-defeating vengeful response—especially from adolescents—by making your relationship the issue. Let the consequences do the teaching.

With young children, the consequences should be as immediate as possible. If after *one* warning, the four- or five-year-old throws the toy again, do a time-out on the spot AND confiscate the toy for a day. Don't warn the child again. The next time the child throws a toy, it gets confiscated immediately. Both parents and children need to remember that first rule—*Follow directions first time!* When you give repeated warnings, you're saying that you forgot (or don't care about) the rule, too, and that your expectations of your child are very low. And, as we stressed earlier, you're also training your child to tune you out.

With much older children and adolescents, stick to short-term consequences and make them relevant to the child's choice. Don't impose "restrictions" that last weeks or months. For many kids long restrictions are the equivalent of life sentences: since they've already lost "everything," kids reason, they may as well do whatever they want because there's nothing left to lose. This empties all your consequences of power. It also turns you into the ogre that you're trying hard not to be by once again effectively changing the subject from the consequences of *their* choice to *your* "meanness." If you want your child to see the world in terms of choice and their own basic goodness, begin early with simple and immediate consequences and never make enforcing consequences personal.

And, again, watch your language. Don't even jokingly make remarks like "The punishment needs to fit the severity of the crime." Whether serious or just kidding, don't ever equate your child's unacceptable behavior with criminal behavior.

Actions Speak Louder than Words

Children's safety and security rely on double standards that allow adults to do things that children are not allowed to do. But there is a more insidious kind of double standard according to which adults sometimes engage in behaviors that children experience as hypocritical or inconsistent. In the following examples, parental behavior communicates values or standards that contradict what has been verbally conveyed.

- Even though the parents have a "No food or drink in the car" rule, Mom brings her morning coffee along as she drives the kids to school
- Hitting to stop a child from hitting another child
- Taking young children to PG-13 movies or letting children go alone to R-rated movies
- Taking a child without shoes or a top into a store with a sign saying Shoes and Shirts Required
- Rolling through a stop sign or a red light
- Not wearing a seatbelt when the law requires it
- Not wearing a seatbelt while requiring one's children to wear them
- Allowing a child to ride in the front seat when prohibited by law (or when the child is shorter than permitted by law)
- Crossing the street without holding a child's hand, when the family rule is "Always hold hands when crossing the street"
- Smoking when "everyone" knows that smoking can kill you
- Drinking alcohol while driving
- Using profanity while punishing children for doing so
- Lying by telling a caller that your spouse isn't home when he or she just doesn't want to talk to the person

We saw in chapters 7 and 8 how many parents treat children, especially little children, as if they were totally oblivious to adult behavior. Not only can this kind of treatment promote dissociative behavior and attentional difficulties, it can also undermine the very values you are trying to impart to your child.

Because children are Technicality Meisters, every time you engage in any behavior like those listed above, they receive your clear behavioral message that rules are there to be broken and that you don't really believe in them. Don't be misled by the fact that *some* children manage to mind rules in spite of parental models to the contrary. Many children soak up the values that are implicit in parental behavior at the expense of the very sincere lessons that parents try to teach.

Behavioral Commentaries

A child's behavior can be a commentary just as much as if it were spoken. But such behavioral commentaries may be harder to recognize. For example, a young child might put on his seatbelt, only to take it off when he notices that his parent doesn't put hers on. The child might comply with a second order to "Put it on!" only to take it off again when he notices that, again, the parent fails to wear hers. Or a teenager may drink alcoholic beverages—and leave surprisingly sloppy evidence that he's drinking—in a household where one or more parents use illegal substances like marijuana or use prescription drugs inappropriately. In the case of the younger child especially, the richness of the child's observational skills and his understanding of the meaning of rules *for adults* goes unrecognized when behavioral commentary behavior is seen as "mere disobedience." Thus children often engage in what we call *parallel rule-breaking* as a way to communicate "If you can do it, I can do it." This is not mere copying, mere imitation. There is an implicit judgment that is masked by the apparent similarity of the child's or adolescent's behavior. Some children and adolescents are quite conscious of what they're doing and what they're tying to communicate. Others aren't.

Clear Communication Requires Making Clear Choices

If you really care about the kind of choices your child makes, you will have to take your own choices seriously.

Jean complained to her friend that her four boys were constantly fighting. When did the fights tend to occur, her friend asked. "Well, it gets very physical," Jean replied, "and it usually starts when they're playing some sort of competitive game." One day not long after this exchange, Jean invited her friend and her husband and seven-year-old to be their guests at the local professional hockey game. Her friend replied that while she really appreciated the invitation, she didn't think it was such a good idea. When Jean expressed surprise and wanted to know why, her friend asked her to describe the players' behavior. Jean replied that most nights there was at least one fight, sometimes many. And sometimes very bad fights. Jean's friend suggested that her hockey-playing sons "should probably not be routinely watching grown men breaking rules and beating the crap out of one another." Jean reluctantly agreed. "Yes, I guess so," Jean replied, "but they love going to the game so much!"

Parents also often find it difficult to "deprive" their children of enjoyable activities. Combine the logic of language with the mild sense of guilt for "taking away" an enjoyable activity and you have a brilliant formula for irrational behavior. Yet parents need to really choose, *and choose quite consciously and deliberately*, between the contradictory values communicated by their verbal injunctions not to fight and the implicit acceptance of blood brawls at the hockey rink.

The more parents are aware of how they may inadvertently promote values they really do not choose to hold, the easier it will be to deal with issues of personal responsibility.

Whose Responsibility?

- "My parents won't let me go to the prom."
- "I can't come out and play today because my mom's mad at me."
- "The movie's off because my dad jerked my keys."
- "My sister got me in trouble, so I can't go to Little League tonight."
- "My mom took away my bike. That's why I can't go riding."
- "My dad won't let me watch TV."
- "My parents won't let me play video games for a week."

Sound familiar? Each of these children or adolescents lost a privilege as a consequence for behavior that was entirely under their control, yet each uses language that assigns responsibility to someone else and makes them the passive victim of someone else's choices. As we stressed in the last chapter, one of the best ways to avoid this flight from responsibility is not to give the child or adolescent the opportunity to blame you by changing the subject to how mean and unfair you are (as evidenced by your angry, punitive tone of voice). But it's also important to correct the language. Billy can't go out and play today because he didn't fulfill an obligation or because he did something he wasn't supposed to do—not because his mom's mad at him. And it's not that Fred's dad won't let him watch TV. It's that Fred lost his TV-watching privileges as a consequence for what he did or didn't do.

Making the Link Between Choice and Consequence Obvious

Sometimes it helps to make the link between behavior and consequences quite clear. One way to do this with younger children is to take away TV-watching time (assuming that you are allowing your children to watch TV). But when, as a consequence, you take five minutes off a particular program, *take it off the end of the program, not the beginning.* Everyone knows that little is lost from the overall effect of a story if you come in shortly after the beginning. But losing out on the ending makes it feel like you've lost out on the entire story. So take time off the end, not the beginning, of TV shows. (This may sound wimpy, but we've found that children find it easier to give up an entire favorite TV show than to be forced to miss the ending. Besides, it's better overall strategy to begin with small consequences and increase bit by bit than to start out with big consequences that force you to make even bigger increases too early in the game.)

For children who are very money-conscious, you can use money as a consequence. We don't think children should be paid for doing chores because helping out is simply part of being a family. If, however, parents do wish to give their children an allowance—say, one hundred pennies for a four-year-old—then they can *take away* a penny every time their child *chooses* not to follow directions. Or a nickel for every hit. This makes it perfectly clear that the losses are not due to parents being mean or punitive; they are due to the child's own personal choices.

"That's all well and good," you may be thinking, "but *my* kid may decide that it's actually worth a nickel to hit his brother." Yes, that may be, and there certainly are adults who think it's worth the ticket to park wherever they want. But they're a very small minority, and, besides, remember that we're talking about little kids. We doubt seriously that many of the "it's worth it to me" illegal parkers had parents with the patience and tenacity that we hope that you will have if your child falls into that category. And remember as well that this little tactic is not meant as a stand-alone technique. Don't forget everything else we've focused on up until now.

So, as the child makes progress, just up the ante. If you began with a consequence of losing a nickel for each time the child hits, raise it to a dime. Be sure that you make it clear in a perfectly matter-of-fact way that the child is 100 percent in control of keeping or losing her money so that she can't say that it's you, the parent, who is taking away the money. Instead, the stress is on the child's ability to keep or lose it solely on the basis of choice. And since our expectation is always that the child will choose to be her real, terrific, good self, we fully expect the child to finish the week with all of her money.

This little technique is to be used *in addition to*, not instead of, other consequences. If the rule is that being allowed to take gymnastics or participate in team sports like soccer depends upon behavior, then you enforce your preexisting consequence *and* the child loses the amount of money you have decided corresponds to the bad choice. Otherwise, you'll hear, "Yeah, but I got to go to soccer anyway!"

If a five-year-old loses all of his one hundred pennies in the first four days of the week, then whatever he loses during the rest of the week comes out of next week's pennies. This may keep some children in the hole for a few weeks, so prepare yourself NOT to feel sorry for them if this happens—otherwise the child will logically conclude that you don't really agree with what you're doing. Or they may assume that you must have something to feel sorry about, which then makes the whole thing about *you* and not about them.

Some hard-headed children, even the very young, will try to make you return to your old pattern of giving up because it doesn't seem to be "working," so don't give up or give in. And be careful that you don't fall for the financial equivalent of "that [spanking] doesn't hurt" and conclude prematurely that your child simply doesn't care about money. (Some kids genuinely don't care about money, but their parents are usually well aware of this before considering this kind of tool.)

Accidents, Mistakes, and Choices

Adults routinely refer to their own bad choices and those of others as "mistakes," a pattern quickly picked up by three-year-olds with radar ears. By three and a half, most children can be heard to say, "I'm sorry. I made a mistake."

Mistakes and choices are as different as accidents and choices. When Sally's mom unknowingly picked up her daughter's new felt name tag and threw it into the washer, she ruined the name tag *by mistake*. She didn't do it on purpose. In this sense, mistakes and accidents have the same meaning—something unintended. But even here, Mom can explain to Sally that *a good choice could have prevented the mistake*. Had Sally's mom chosen to sort through the items in the laundry basket as she usually does, she would have found Sally's name tag mixed in with the items that were supposed to be washed. But, because she chose to rush and not to pay attention, Sally's mom mistakenly washed something that was never supposed to get wet.

While parents struggle to clarify these distinctions, the media amplify the confusion. Public officials in front of cameras and microphones are routinely apologizing for their past "mistakes" when it is perfectly clear that they knowingly chose to do what they did. With a little help, even young children can understand that adults, too, try to escape taking full personal responsibility for their choices by labeling them "mistakes."

Intended Acts with Unintended Outcomes

Susie and Cindy have been picking at each other all afternoon—with Susie doing most of the picking. Finally, sick and tired of being followed around the house, Cindy turns to her sister and says, "Leave me alone!" then abruptly pushes her sister backward. Unprepared for the push, Susie loses her balance and falls, hitting her head on the sharp corner of the metal and glass end table.

Cindy screams as blood flows from the back of her sister's head and her mother comes running. "I didn't mean to push her!"

"What did you do to your sister?" the girls' mother says. "WHAT DID YOU DO?"

"I didn't mean to push her, I really didn't!"

At times like this, parents often take advantage of what has happened to impress upon their children that pushing can be very dangerous. But there's a further distinction the parent can make that addresses the issue of personal agency and responsibility and not just the dangerousness of the behavior. In this case, the girls' mom can explain to both of her daughters that, even though Cindy's response to her sister was a heated reaction, *it was still a choice*. Cindy didn't push her sister "by accident," as she might have had she herself tripped and fallen into her sister. Nor did she push her sister "by mistake," as she might have done had she turned around and pushed her, thinking that Susie was a door that needed shutting.

Moments like this offer parents the opportunity to say to their children, "Yes, you did. You *did* mean to push your sister. What you *didn't* mean was for your sister to get hurt. So, the next time someone bugs you, teases you, follows you around, or even tries to push *you*, DON'T REACT like that. Don't push back. It's too dangerous. It's too easy for someone to get hurt, maybe very, very badly. The way to make sure that nobody gets hurt because of what you choose to do is *to make good choices*. Come get me the next time you feel like pushing your sister. Let the adult who's around take care of it."

11

Mad, Bad, and Sad:
How Communication Shapes Emotion,
Aggression, and Relatedness

Our understanding of what anger is and what can be done about it has been powerfully shaped by language. Listen to the expressions we use to describe anger. Anger makes us *boil, steam, fume, blow up, seethe,* and *burst.* Anger *wells up, builds up, rises,* and *erupts.* We work to *suppress anger, keep it in,* or *hold it down.* Or we talk about *ventilating anger, getting it out, letting it out, pouring it out, blowing it off,* or *letting out steam.* Otherwise, we try to *hold it in, hold it down, suppress it,* or *put a lid on it.*

These expressions correspond to feelings. When we're really angry or, worse yet, in a rage, *it feels as if* we're bursting at the seams. It feels as if anger's in there and has to get out. We may get *red in the face* and others may tell us *not to get so hot* or *not to get overheated.* But as much as language corresponds to, and doubtless grew out of, our bodily experience of emotion, the words and expressions are very misleading. When we're angry, we ARE angry. Anger is not really inside us.

Unfortunately, a tradition of thousands of years of linguistic convention and the folk psychology reflected in everyday language was given a boost of "scientific" respectability by Sigmund Freud's curious models of "instincts," "drives," and emotions. In Freud's model, it's as if when you push down on an imaginary cylinder that contains anger, the anger pushes up somewhere else—just like fluid in a closed system. According to this "mental hydraulics" model, you can't really make anger go away. All you can do is to put it somewhere else. Or try to "get it out."

The reason for this widespread mistaken notion is that people routinely confuse two very different categories—communication and emotion. We use the same words to refer to two very different behaviors. When we tell someone to "get your feelings *out*, you'll feel better," we mean simply that the process of communication with another person (a relationship) will improve how the person feels. There is a sense of freedom and connectedness in being able to express oneself verbally to another person, to cry on someone's shoulder, or to be held. And when one person facilitates another's communication, the results are instantaneous. However, when people talk about "getting anger out," they tend to mean so literally, as if there were X amount of anger that had to be released. Rarely do you hear someone say, "Just tell me calmly and quietly that you are angry and your anger will be gone." No, people commonly think that anger is somewhere "inside" and that one must try literally to "get it out" through very physical means, such as screaming, pounding on punching bags, or breaking things.

It's here that we can see what words have done to us. Just where is this anger that has to be "got out"? Is it "inside" somewhere? If so, where? There are, of course, no good answers to these silly questions because anger isn't anywhere. And you can't "get it out" because there's no place "inside" where it "is." We don't have "anger bladders." That's why attempts to "get it out" become self-perpetuating.

We, as therapists, discovered many years ago that the best-intentioned efforts to get anger out routinely backfire. Anger breeds anger. That's why angry children in therapy go on for years just "getting it out," when they really should have been changing, and changing quickly—like real children can. Debbie asked a five-year-old, who didn't sleep well and had been told by a previous therapist to "beat up your pillow, not your brother," how he thought his pillow felt. "I think it wants to hit me back!" he said. We already know that children are logical little creatures who live in a world of intensely personal meaning. If you want your child to be able to put his head down on his pillow and sleep, don't encourage him to put all his anger there! The traditional "anger release" gimmicks such as punching bags, sock-em clowns, and other dead-end get-your-anger-out devices tend to *increase*, not decrease, anger and aggression.

Anger Is Dangerous

A number of years ago a colleague told us about a nearby inpatient alcohol and addictions program that used "anger groups" as part of its treatment approach. In these groups, which are very common in many recovery programs, group members are encouraged to "get their true feelings out" and to express the emotions that they have tended to "repress" or "hold in." Participants in this particular group had become very impatient with one group member, a man in his fifties who insisted that his emotions belonged to him and that he "wasn't sharing them with a bunch of strangers." The group made it their goal to get their hold-out member to express his emotions. It wasn't long until nearly every minute of group time was devoted to the one member's "resistance." After a week or so of being the constant object of the group's attention, the man finally stood up, fuming. "You want me to get angry?" he said, seething. "You wanna see what anger really is?" he boiled. "Well, I'll show you!" he screamed—and dropped dead. Right in the middle of the group. Sad to say, no lessons were learned, and the "anger groups" continue to this day.

As the title of one book on the subject puts it, *Anger Kills*. Far from being a great solution to human problems, anger only breeds more anger. Anger raises the blood pressure and is bad for the heart. In fact, it's so counterproductive that the only time we ever actually try to mobilize anger is in the case of children who are so afraid of their own anger that they express almost no negative emotion at all. But these children are the exception even in a busy practice. Most children naturally express frustration and anger, so there is no need for parents to promote its expression.

Mad and Bad

Anger isn't the only emotion subject to confusion. What is the most common symbol used to designate "bad behavior" by schoolteachers, special education personnel, and mental health professionals? When a first grader tells us that he got in trouble in school today, under what symbol on the board does he tell us his teacher put his name? And what symbol for "bad behavior" do we see drawn or stamped on "behavior modification cards" or "behavior report cards"? Something clearly and unequivocally "bad"? No. This is what we see:

That's right: a *sad* face.

Given what we've already learned about logical, literal childhood thinking, what effect should we expect this SAD = BAD equivalency to have on children, especially young children?

Just think about the average first-grade classroom in this country. Since roughly half of marriages end in divorce these days, it's reasonable to expect that a great many of the children in the average first-grade class will have a real, bona fide reason to be sad. Now, if you can get your name put up under the sad face by engaging in "bad" behavior, it's only logical that a significant number of children, especially the most literal-minded, would unconsciously identify with this symbol, even to the point of behaving badly in order to get their name under the sad face.

We've asked a number of teachers in the early elementary grades to quietly replace the sad face with a very small "Grrr" face to see what happens.

As expected, the overall behavior of the students improved without the teacher saying a single word to her class about the symbol change.

We must admit, however, that it can be discouraging to see sad faces used to represent "bad" behavior at almost every turn. If you want to make sure that your child's environment isn't (inadvertently but still literally) pulling for bad behavior, take this issue to your child's classroom, the PTA, or even your local school board.

Mad and Sad

Every parent, indeed every adult who has ever spent time with a child, has seen what happens when anger and sadness get confused. Probably the most familiar example is the tearful tantrum. Although tears may be flowing copiously, tantrums aren't really about sadness. They're about anger, frustration, and even rage. Although they often look alike, anger and sadness are really very different.

Anger is a distancing emotion. Anger pushes people away. Sadness, on the other hand, is an affiliative emotion. It draws people nearer. (About the only time anger unites is in communal revenge, and that's something we're working on discouraging, not encouraging.)

Anger is either the expression of a lack of vulnerability or a denial of vulnerability. The loneliness and vulnerability of the bully are not hard to perceive just beneath the surface hostility and off-putting (distancing) behavior. Genuine sadness, on the other hand, requires of both sides of the relationship a willingness to tolerate vulnerability.

Anger and Emotional Accessibility

Angry kids are inaccessible kids. Who would want to get close to them? Whether such anger reflects a longstanding style or a context-dependent reaction, its effect is to push away. (The same, of course, is true for adults.)

Whenever we work with an angry, mean, threatening, or off-putting child or adolescent, the first thing we try to do is to convert the anger into sadness. Even in the first history-taking encounter with parents and child, we are on the lookout for opportunities. If a child screams that he "hates" his brother and then adds, "Besides, he never even plays with me!" we say how sad it is that his brother won't involve him in his games. If a child erupts into a rage because his Lego creation won't hold together, we tell him that it's okay to be sad that he couldn't get it to stand up on its own.

Changing Anger Is Not Failing to Accept the Child

Some parents say, "But shouldn't we be validating his anger? If we don't acknowledge the anger, aren't we really refusing to accept him for who he is?" Sure, IF that's who you want him to be. But you have more choice in the matter than you might think. As for validating anger, there's no need—anger is self-validating. An angry child knows he's piping mad, and it's not long until everyone else does, too. What the angry child doesn't know, however, is that there is sadness lying just beneath the emotional surface. And he or she may never know it, and may never experience it, if you don't facilitate the transition. And don't worry: changing angry, frustrated, or enraged reactions into sadness won't prevent your child from *telling* you about anger in an appropriate manner.

Preschool teachers and daycare providers, whose environments tend to be much more active and emotion-filled than elementary school classrooms, have told us that they have been amazed how much they can lower the aggression-revenge index just by redefining angry responses in terms of sadness. These workers have found that responding to a child's anger and desire to hurt back with an empathetic remark such as "It's so sad that your beautiful building got knocked down" can often calm the angry reaction, thereby heading off the retaliatory response. Over time, the child internalizes the adult's definition of the experience and changes his response style. A preschool classroom in which adults routinely redefine traditionally angry responses in terms of sadness and disappointment tends to be a calmer and less aggressive environment. Just as in the clinical setting, such an environment tends to be much more conducive to whatever educational or therapeutic work needs to be done.

Integrative and Disintegrative Emotions

We have worked with many angry, reactive, impulsive, and klutzy children over the years whose behavior, including gross and fine motor coordination, improved markedly as we helped them deal with sadness. Why? Because emotions serve as a kind of modulator or governor for integrative behaviors such as reason, judgment, planning, and even motor behavior. Yet even many physicians and therapists who are aware of the role of the frontal lobes of the brain in modulating integrative behavior often believe that only time and maturity, i.e., frontal lobe development, will make these integrative behaviors possible—and so they don't try to change them. And yet everyday language tells us that it's very hard to do anything well when you're angry.

Anger is a *disintegrative* emotion, whereas sadness is an *integrative* emotion. "Just calm down," we tell someone who is so upset they can't do something. "Just calm down and you'll get it." So remove expressions like "I know that makes you angry" or "That really makes you angry, doesn't it" from your vocabulary. Such expressions only reinforce the very behavior that you are trying to change. Instead, just say "You're sad. That hurt. Don't worry, you'll get it!"

Missing the Forest of Sadness for the Trees of Anger

Willy was a four-year-old with cerebral palsy whose oppositionalism, defiance, and frequent temper tantrums his parents simply took for granted. When everyone was looking, Willy was syrupy sweet to his little sister, but when no one was looking, he would hit or kick her or push her baby carrier over. We met Willy shortly after he was discovered in the act of trying to push his sister's baby carrier—with her inside—off a table.

Actually, it was Willy's mother and *stepfather* who decided to act. And it was actually his *half-sister* toward whom he was so aggressive. Willy's divorced father had little to do with him, and when he could be pressured into taking Willy for visitation, he largely ignored the boy and called him names like "retard" and "stupid." The father felt no real obligation toward his son and paid no child support on the grounds that his ex-wife had "married money."

Willy's appearance was deceiving. While he was extremely disabled, he was actually very bright. We could see this in his ability to do very complex things. For example, to bug his parents (mother and stepfather), he would steal the TV remote control and sit on it. When his parents had searched long enough, Willy would then change channels by moving his rear end and then burst into laughter when his parents figured out what he had done.

But, as bright as Willy was, he was no match for his baby sister. Since she was not yet toilet trained, no one got mad at her when she wet or soiled her diaper. Much more was expected of Willy because he was four.

It wasn't fair. And it wasn't fair that this baby of a sister could speak clearly and effortlessly while Willy had to struggle to articulate the simplest of words. And it really wasn't fair that she had two full-time parents who never called her names and who were always there for her. No one had even realized how tragic and how poignant Willy's situation was because he kept the family in constant turmoil. Nor had anyone discerned Willy's sadness about being so much less adept than his baby sister because the sadness was masked by his devious and diabolical meanness toward her.

With our help, as Willy allowed himself to feel profoundly sad that his father didn't really care about him, and sad that everything was so excruciatingly difficult for him, his behavior changed dramatically. His relationship with his sister warmed genuinely and the aggression decreased in frequency and severity. Allowing himself to feel sad about his condition and his lot in life allowed Willy to stop feeling like he deserved the cruel name-calling and lack of attention from his father. Feeling sad about his lot in life also made it easier for Willy to see that his "bad" hearing, "bad" coordination, and "bad" speech (articulation) didn't mean that *he* was bad. All of this was more or less to be expected. But what was dramatically striking was a small but genuine improvement in Willy's motor coordination.

As we said, anger is a *disintegrative* emotion, as is its close cousin, frustration. When you help someone, like Willy, to move from anger to sadness, you actually remove blocks to integrative functioning.

Anger and Taking Control of Dyscontrol

We have seen many young children, mostly boys, who were thought to have some sort of pervasive developmental disorder affecting their cognitive and motor development. Klutzy, and often with speech problems, these children tend to seem unfocused and impulsive. Typically, the behavior of these children had been explained to the parents in terms of "mood swings" (we have seen two-and-a-half-year-olds diagnosed with

Manic Depressive Illness and treated with lithium) and Attention Deficit Disorder (for which stimulants like Ritalin, Dexedrine, and Adderall were routinely prescribed). In fact, many of these children had been assigned multiple diagnoses and many were taking a handful of different medications. The anger outbursts and oppositional-defiant behavior, their parents were told, were simply part of the whole syndrome.

The Three Stooges Syndrome

The closer we looked at these children, the more fascinating they became. Often their disordered and apparently confused behavior coalesced and became more focused and purposeful in response to a firm but gentle approach and the highly structured space of the playtherapy room. What we saw in the play of these children was very different from what everyone saw in their everyday behavior. And the most striking aspect of what we saw was their intelligence, perceptual acuity, and detail-mindedness.

The behavior we were seeing resulted from a disparity between what these young children (boys especially) knew they *should* be able to do and their actual ability to accomplish these motor tasks—from speaking to moving about. They were like characters in a science fiction story, complex minds stuck in little bodies that they couldn't make perform as they wanted. The children with the garbled speech had routinely been judged to be "language-disordered," yet their actual language skills were perfectly intact. Their *internal* language was not only normal, it was often more complex and more refined than one would expect for their age. What was lacking was the ability to put it to work with words: their speech (a motor skill) lagged way behind their ability to think and use language, resulting in immense frustration. As we all know, out of immense frustration real anger is born.

The more predominantly klutzy children—those with gross motor control problems—inspired our description of what these children do in response to their inability to control their own motor behavior. This is what we call the *Three Stooges Syndrome.* The Three Stooges are always getting hurt—*but at least they're in charge of it!*

In order to gain some semblance of control over their poor gross motor coordination, these children *take control of dyscontrol.* If the four-year-old bangs into the child's table on entering the playtherapy room, he'll go one step further and overturn it. If he knocks a part off his Lego structure while reaching for another toy, he'll topple the whole thing. If he trips on the rug, he won't just stumble, he'll fall and thrash around all over the place. It's as if the child is saying through his behavior "It's not that I couldn't help bumping into that table, I knocked it over on purpose." Even though the end result is infinitely more embarrassing, and even though it actually calls far more humiliating attention to the child than the initial coordination mishap, at least it feels to the child as if he's in charge.

It's extremely important to get to the sadness and sense of powerlessness and dyscontrol in these children's experience because it's often possible to improve things significantly.

We've found that many of these children literally hate the part of their body that won't work the way they want it to. We reassure them that they don't have a "bad" mouth if they can't yet speak clearly or if they can't even get the proper words out. And we tell them, with the most genuine compassion that we can muster, that it's so sad that they can't yet make their body work like they want it to, and that they must not hurt themselves. Because of the disintegrative effect of anger and the integrative effect of sadness on both cognitive and motor functions, sometimes simply decreasing the anger and increasing the genuine sadness is all it takes to bring about a significant increase in motor coordination. This can sometimes interrupt the horrible vicious cycle—anger, self-sabotage, self-punishment, exaggerated motor dyscontrol, negative self-image, and revenge on the world—which, not surprisingly, makes everything better.

In other cases, changing the anger and exaggerated dyscontrol into sadness allows the child to ride out what is often the relatively short time necessary for his motor control to catch up with his mind. It's very important to access the sadness and to interrupt the self-humiliating behavior because even children who would have eventually "grown out" of such behavior can develop an otherwise avoidable lifelong personality style. (When this happens, it also skews our understanding of what's "inborn," "genetic," and "unchangeable.")

America's Cruelest Home Videos

Even though slapstick and animation are obviously not real—even to most little children—we advise parents not to let their children watch movies, cartoons, and television shows designed to make us laugh at people hurting other people. Such programs are an open invitation for young children to imitate what they see on the screen. One television show, however, *America's Funniest Home Videos*, goes far beyond the make-believe of cartoons and slapstick and shows home videos of people really getting hurt or really hurting others. People of all ages, from toddlers to the elderly, fall down, fall off vehicles or buildings, run into things or into other people. One video shows a man attempting to mount a balance beam—and landing instead on his genitals. The audience roars with laughter and is invited to laugh even harder at these cruelly painful scenes. If you don't want your child to see hilarity in human suffering, and if you do want your child to develop a genuine sense of empathy and caring for others, make such programs off-limits and talk openly with your child about the fact that such pain and suffering are NOT funny.

Anger as Failed Communication

It's important to be on the lookout for children's aggression as failed communication. When a child hits or kicks a parent, or when a child screams insults or even "I hate you!" at a parent, anger and pain are certainly communicated, *but there is no communicative content.* Even the horrible "I hate you!" tells a parent nothing that he or she can do anything about. Such empty communications are a sign that parent-child communication has broken down and needs attention. At such times, parents need to wonder what the real issues are, what the child is NOT talking about.

Don't Create Opportunities for Empty Communication

One of the first things we do when working with anger and aggression problems in children is to ask the family to suspend all "horseplay." Children often use horseplay—hurting instead of truly communicating—to tell parents that they're mad at them. When this occurs, parents—usually fathers who like to horse around—are confused and upset by the unexpected anger and meanness that comes out of their children.

Fathers are often hesitant to give up "fake wrestling" and horseplay both because they enjoy it and because it allows them to get very close to their children without any significant emotional risk (although they're not usually consciously aware of the latter reason). But these activities make it all too easy for someone to get squeezed just a bit too hard or tickled too long or to feel trapped and powerless—and then hurting back flares up. This ends up feeding a vicious cycle of hurt and hurting back that drowns out real communication possibilities. Every bit of anger-as-empty-communication expressed by children makes it that much less likely that they will actually tell you what they're really thinking or feeling.

What applies to parents applies to siblings as well. If you find the actual level of anger or aggression in the "play" of your two or more children to be too intense, don't accept explanations such as "We're just playing," "We're just pretending," or "We're just fake-wrestling." When one person is angry enough to hurt another, there's always a reason. The reason may not relate directly to that particular person, but there's a reason nonetheless.

The same applies to the "Just kidding!" insolent or aggressive behaviors of children or adolescents. Such "Just kidding!" behavior can also mask unexpressed communication. Parents tend to react to the emotion and lack of respect but typically fail to look deeper for the communicative meaning. Any such behavior is a red flag that should alert you to the likelihood that communication has broken down somewhere.

Listen Carefully for Children's Self-Put-Downs

We caution parents to pay close attention to AND to put a quick end to children's "Oh, what a dunce!" behavior, such as when a child hits himself in the head. Parents will often stop these behaviors when they see them without realizing that that was just the first step. These self-hurtful behaviors are a signal that something's wrong and needs to be addressed. Sometimes, all that is needed is parental understanding, a shift from anger to sadness, and the sort of reorganization that then allows the child to move on productively. At other times, such behavior may be a sign that something is really wrong in the child's life and that the parent should pay much closer attention.

Don't Foil Genuine Spontaneous Sadness

Perhaps because sadness does signal vulnerability, parents have a tendency to try to fix it or make it go away when their child actually does share it with them. If Sam is really sad that his team lost, Mom is likely to try to make him feel better by telling him that he played brilliantly himself. Dad, on the other hand, is likely to explain the mechanics involved, that the other team was "just too good." In either case, neither of Sam's parents really accepts his sadness, thereby discouraging a genuinely healthy response to disappointment. And, as is so often the case, what Sam's logical mind hears is that he is *wrong* to feel as he does.

12

Structure, Rules, and Boundaries

Imagine that you live in the suburbs and work downtown. Every weekday, for years, you've driven to the commuter station, dropped off your car, and taken the train into the city. And every day, like clockwork, the fortyish woman in the business suit with the computer case boards the city-bound train when you do and returns home on the same 5:20 outbound.

Suddenly, one day, the fortyish woman in the business suit with the computer case isn't waiting for the city-bound train when you arrive. The rest of the day, it's hard to concentrate on your work because you keep wondering what could have happened to her. Did she die? Did she move away? Was she a victim of corporate downsizing? She's never been out of work for so much as a sick day. *What could have happened to her?*

Why this obsessive preoccupation with the fortyish woman in the business suit with the computer case? After all, though you may have exchanged a smile a few times over the years, you've never so much as spoken to the woman—and yet you can't get her out of your mind. In fact, you're actually worried about this familiar stranger whose life is as much of a puzzle today as it was the first time you laid eyes on her well over five years ago. So what's going on?

Experience structures life. Consistent experience structures life in a way that affects us deeply—even if, as in the case of your daily train trip with the fortyish woman in the business suit with the computer case, we're not aware of it until the structure disappears.

Every child needs structure, rules, and boundaries, and every child needs the experience of consistency, continuity, and predictability in his or her life. These are the absolutely essential *nonspecific fundamentals* that, like the trellis for the vine, allow the child to build the unique structure of his or her personality and cognitive, emotional, and interpersonal styles.

Caring Minus Consistency
Equals Chaos

It's eight-thirty and time for five-year-old Elizabeth Samuelson to go to bed. It's been a long day—a really good day—with an after-school trip to the hands-on museum and then three or four stores to fill out Elizabeth's new school wardrobe and pick out a present for next week's birthday party sleepover.

"Elizabeth," Becky Samuelson says in a pleasant voice, "it's time for bed, so go get your pajamas on."

Elizabeth has remained in a great mood right through dinner and into the "all inside the lines" coloring she has been doing for the last half hour. "I will," she says as she continues to color.

"It's time to stop coloring NOW," Becky says, this time a bit more forcefully, as she turns the TV off with the remote control.

"Okay, okay!" Elizabeth says. But she continues her meticulous inside-the-lines coloring.

"ELIZABETH!" Becky emphasizes each word. "PUT YOUR COLORS AWAY AND GET READY FOR BED."

"I'm going, I'm going!" Elizabeth shakes her head as if to say "What do you think I am, deaf!" but makes no move to get up and head for her bedroom. Just as Becky is about to get up and escort her daughter into her bedroom, Sam Samuelson looks up from *The Wall Street Journal* he's been reading and says, "Elizabeth, your pajamas"—at which point Elizabeth puts her crayons away and heads off to get ready for bed.

"Why," Becky Samuelson wants to know, "why is it that when *I* tell her to go to bed, she doesn't move? But all her father has to do is say her name, raise his voice—or even *look* at her—and she jumps to do what he says!" Becky pauses, and then adds exasperatedly, "And he's not even an involved dad!" Becky Samuelson assumes that Elizabeth jumps when Dad barks because she's afraid of him. In this case, the "technique" would be in the tone of voice or the volume. Dad's bigger and gruffer and that's why Elizabeth jumps when he raises his voice but not when Mom does. But that's NOT the answer.

While Sam Samuelson may indeed be gruffer or more intimidating, the key to his instantaneous success in getting Elizabeth to follow his directions is to be found, ironically, in Becky's disparaging remark that "he's not even an involved dad!" That's right. And because his actual interventions are few and far between, Sam is actually *much more consistent* than his wife. Since Elizabeth's father tends to intervene at stereotypic moments, his interventions tend to be equally stereotyped. Sam doesn't kid around. And he certainly doesn't repeat himself three, four, or five times. He intervenes once, and that's it.

Becky, on the other hand, spends LOTS of time with her daughter, which provides her with many more opportunities every single day to be inconsistent. Becky doesn't get serious until the third or fourth time, and Elizabeth knows it. All Becky has to do to be as "effective" as her husband is to change her parenting and communication style from caringly inconsistent to caringly consistent. It's as simple as that.

Boundaries

Boundaries are everywhere. Wherever there is an *inside* and an *outside*, there are boundaries. Whatever is inside your skin is you; whatever is outside is not-you. You live inside, the world lives outside. Most families live in the same home. In fact, we know that the nature of a family has changed when part of the family lives in one home and the other part lives in another home. Inside homes, we find rooms and doors. There's Mom and Dad's bedroom and Johnny's bedroom. They're not the same. If Johnny shares a bedroom, there are probably two beds, especially if he shares it with a sister. There's also Mom and Dad's bathroom and Johnny's bathroom. Their boundaries are physically rigid but socially fluid: sometimes it's okay to come in and sometimes it's not. And some boundaries are differential: the family dog or cat can come into the living room but not the family cow.

Space Invaders

It's curious, in a society that is widely convinced that a huge proportion of its members suffer from brain-based disorders of genetic origin affecting attention and impulse control, that almost no one pays any attention to boundaries until they're violated. But once they are, wow! do people get upset!

- "He's LOOKING at me!" screams your five-year-old, sitting on one side of the backseat while his four-year-old brother is a good three feet away. Not a finger has been lifted, not a body touched, not a toy broken—and yet Joey pierces your eardrums with a bloodcurdling scream as loud as if his brother had stabbed him with a pencil.
- "Billy's got his foot inside my door!" screams Brad. To make his invasion even more humiliating and maddening, Billy is wearing his brother's Denver Broncos T-shirt. There will be a battle.
- "Sally put a red Lego on my house!" yells her sister. "Make her take it off!"
- "Stop kicking my seat!" Mom yells as Junior distracts her dangerously while they drive through the most hazardous part of town.

Sound familiar? If you have kids, or just spend time around kids, you know a Space Invader when you see one. Have you noticed that your kids can be absolutely oblivious to you for the entire morning—but as soon as you pick up the telephone, they're clamoring for your time and attention? This is not just a separation issue. Some situations actually seem to invite space invasion.

All Kids Are Space Invaders

All children have to learn what they can touch and what they can't, where they can go and where they can't. As with every aspect of behavior, some children have more compliant styles when it comes to rules and boundaries, while others are headstrong and persistent. Parents who, with gentle firmness, impose boundaries from the very beginning of the child's life, and remain consistent in how they treat boundaries, will have an easier time during their child's growing-up period. Unfortunately, some parents don't realize until quite late in that process that they could have had some constructive input into the development of their child's treatment of structure, rules, and boundaries.

Real Space Invaders Don't Do Well Socially

Real Space Invaders are not typically popular kids. They get into everyone's personal, physical, and emotional space. They get too close. They grab. They touch too much (often, if they're very young, in the form of hitting, kicking, or biting). Space Invaders rarely respect the sanctity of another child's or adult's personal possessions or enclosed spaces (bedrooms, banks, purses, wallets, playthings, etc.). They tease and make fun of other children, the verbal equivalent of ripping someone's clothes off in order to make them feel vulnerable and self-conscious. And, often at very early ages, these little Space Invaders, the male variety usually, seem obsessed with taking things apart. But rarely do they have any interest in putting the clock, the radio, or the telephone back together again. (Children who actually try to put the disassembled items back together again are not real Space Invaders but future engineers.)

Because Space Invaders tend to alienate other children, they can become loners. As you can imagine, this, in turn, results in a vicious cycle in which they become brilliant at preemptively pushing people away, heading off rejection by making sure it takes place.

Lack of respect for personal space in a four-year-old Space Invader is annoying. In a sixteen-year-old seated behind the wheel of a two-ton vehicle, it can be fatal. (The way to cure "road rage," by the way, is not to turn it into yet another psychiatric "disorder" but to deal with these

Space Invaders before they ever get their hands on the wheel of a potentially lethal weapon called a car.)

Real Space Invaders Don't Do Well Academically

Space Invaders are much more than impulsive and inattentive. *They don't respect boundaries.* This lack of sensitivity to, and respect for, boundaries is extremely important, but it is rarely recognized or appreciated as such because explanatory theories of currently popular disorders like ADHD and "learning disabilities" focus on impulse control, not on boundary relations.

Here's an exchange that took place toward the beginning of our clinical work together. A single, working mom brought in her seven-year-old second-grade nonreader who was referred for help with the "behavioral component" of his "learning disabilities." Dad was long gone by this point, and the mom, who dropped out of school at the end of the ninth grade, had to work three different jobs to make ends meet. Despite her lack of education, this mom was quite bright.

After Debbie and the child had left Denis's office for the playtherapy room, Denis asked the mom, "What's a word?"

"What do you mean, 'What's a word?' "

"I mean, how do you know a word when you see one? How can you tell what's a word and what's not?"

The mom shrugged her shoulders.

"Okay, here, take a look at this book." Denis handed her an old Soviet French-Russian literary dictionary from a nearby shelf. He opened the

---

66. passer l'eau et le feu pour... пойти в огонь и в воду за...:

— Je suis bien aise de vous rencontrer, dit-elle d'un ton résolu. Vous êtes un honnête homme, vous allez me conduire. Je remets mon sort entre vos mains...
— Me voilà, madame, prêt à **passer l'eau et le feu pour** vous et avec vous (*G. Sand, «Horace»*).
— Я очень рада, что встретила вас, — сказала она решительно. — Вы порядочный человек, я пойду за вами. Моя судьба в ваших руках...
— С вами и ради вас, сударыня, я готов в огонь и в воду.

dictionary to a particular page and pointed to a Russian translation of a French literary excerpt. "Show me a word," Denis urged as he pointed to the paragraph.

"I don't know," the mom replied. "I can't read that. What is it anyway, Russian?" The mom laughed, then said, "Okay, that's a word," as she pointed to a word meaning "fate."

"Now, how can you tell that's a word?" Denis asked.

"Well, I dunno . . . 'cause it's separate from the others."

"That's right. There's a *space* between it and the preceding word and between it and the word that follows. It doesn't matter whether it's in Russian, French, or English, you can recognize words because they're *boundaried*: they're boundaried off by a space before and after them. Okay, now show me a sentence." The mom hesitated, then pointed to the sentence beginning with what she called "the backwards *R*" and ending with a period. At this point the mom agreed that we can all recognize sentences because they, too, have a recognizable *structure* and they, too, are boundaried—typically by a capital letter and a punctuation mark. She also agreed that she could recognize a paragraph in Russian because Russian paragraphs also have a recognizable *structure*—even paragraphs made up of "words with weird and backwards letters." They, too, follow certain *rules*, and they, too, are *boundaried*. At this point, Denis asked the mom if she agreed that, in order to be able to read, a child has to perceive, recognize, and RESPECT structures, rules, and boundaries.

"Yeah, sure," said the mom. "That makes sense."

"Well," Denis asked, "does *your child* respect structure, rules, and boundaries?"

"Are you kidding! Gimme a break!"

"Does he respect your personal space? Does he follow the rules at home or at school?"

"Absolutely not!"

"So why should he be successful at reading?"

"Well," said the mom, "I guess he shouldn't!"

The Experiential Requisites of Learning

Ask yourself this simple question: *What aspect of in-class work, homework, or learning in general is NOT dependent upon structure, rules, and bounda-*

ries? First children have to go to school. Then, most of the time, they have to stay in their seats and out of their desks, their neighbor's space, or the lovely view out the window. You can analyze every single aspect of normal everyday school activities in terms of structure, rules, and boundaries—from the child's seat to the sentence on the page of the reader facing him on his desktop.

Commonsense Approaches to Common Problems

Clearly, it doesn't make any sense at all to set off on a wild goose chase for mythical brain disorders when parents have it within their power to use structure, rules, and boundaries to shape their child's cognitive-behavioral and biobehavioral styles. But most children, regardless of socioeconomic status, intelligence, or even creativity, *do* need help recognizing and minding boundaries. While most parents simply take this for granted when their children are infants and early toddlers, they seem to fall victim to the mistaken belief that the greater autonomy and independence of childhood means that it's safe to ease up on structure, rules, and boundaries. The arrival of a new baby, whose need for structure and boundaries is intense, can also turn parents' attention away from older children. Whatever the cause, this lapse can come at significant cost.

Put Structure Back into the Picture and Get a Structured Kid

While it's great to have been consistent from the very beginning, at any point in their child's life parents can put structure, rules, and boundaries back into the picture. In fact, that's just what we do with impulsive, oppositional, spacey nonreaders. We certainly *don't* do remedial educational tutoring. In fact, it's extremely rare that we even recommend private tutoring. Instead, we simply deal with the issues affecting the child's life—his absent, nonsupporting, uncaring father, his overworked, exhausted, and often impatient mother, and his horrible self-image in the face of embarrassing school failure—just as we would with any child living through similar experiences. At the same time, we help his mom to institute, or reinstate, the structure, rules, and boundaries the child is lacking and to maintain them with the consistency and continuity that will generate some much-needed positive predictability in the child's world. What happens? Nearly all of these children start reading (or doing math, getting better grades, fewer notes home, etc.).

The moral of the story? It's never too late to establish and maintain reasonable structure, rules, and boundaries.

Respect for Rules

Respect is an interesting word, and words can be great teachers. To see deeply into the meaning of *respect*, and to learn the simple but profound lessons it has to teach, just divide it in half. What do you get? *Re-spect: to look twice* (from the Latin *re + specere*, "to look"). What do we—and little children—see when we look twice at how adults treat the rules and boundaries they want children to perceive, respect, and mind?

- Parents who don't call their home-alone teenagers to let them know that they have arrived safely in another city even though they have a "Call when you get there" rule for their kids.
- Parents who snack on dinner preparations, having just told the kids, "No snacks before dinner!"
- Parents complaining about the kids' prolonged phone calls when they spend half the afternoon talking to their best friend across town—or tying up the phone line while on the Internet.
- Parents who give young children alcohol at a restaurant "because it's a special occasion."
- Parents who drive faster than the speed limit because "that's a dumb limit for this part of town."
- Parents who unfasten their airplane seatbelts even though the Fasten Seatbelt sign is illuminated and the captain just announced a period of very bad turbulence.
- Parents who smoke in the nonsmoking section of the restaurant.

From the very beginning of this book, we have stressed that adults routinely fail to realize the difference between *conventional meaning*—what they want and intend to communicate—and the literal meaning of the words they use. We began with words because language is the very essence of what it means to be human. But behavior communicates as surely, as powerfully, and *as subtly* as do words. And the fact is, parents, and adults in general, routinely break the rules and violate the boundaries they want their children to respect. Again, it's like variations on a theme. Adults break the rules they want their children to follow and violate the boundaries they want their children to respect in every conceivable manner. They do so over and over, day after day, month after month, year after year.

The very fact that expressions such as "Do as I say, not as I do" exist reminds us of the transparency of everyday language and behavior. Adults seem to believe that massive, but subtle, double standards and that striking, but subtle, inconsistency in their words, in their behavior, and in the values their words and behavior reflect are totally without effect. Adults really do treat children—the most intricate, detailed, and powerful data-processing instruments in the known universe—as if they were deaf and blind.

If you really want to take seriously the powerful potential of children's development, you will have to be much more aware of how your own mundane failure to follow rules and respect boundaries shapes the very mind you are trying to protect and support. In our clinical work, we find it infinitely easier to deal with horrible acute crises, from child abuse to unexpected deaths, than to try to counter the effects of the subtle, constant, relentless undermining of basic values implicit in parental inconsistency and everyday rule-breaking. Acute crises are best, and most easily, solved acutely. The subtly chronic nature of everyday parental inconsistency and contradiction is much more of a challenge.

"Exceptions to the Rule" Work Only When They Are Genuinely Exceptions

Exceptions are about *contrast*. Many of the examples in the list of mundane rule-breaking and boundary violations above can be found in a single household, often in the behavior of a single parent. Though each of our examples may not be "serious in itself," the *cumulative effect defines a pattern of values*. It is the everyday pattern of such attitudes and behaviors that determines the foundational or baseline set of "family values"—not what the parents say or how many times they go to church, the synagogue, or the mosque.

If you don't routinely speed up to just barely make it through yellow lights, and if you don't routinely roll through stop signs, your child will understand when you cautiously drive through a red light on your way to the emergency room with a critically injured family member. If you don't hit your child, your child will hear "No hitting!" much differently than if you do. If you don't bring your coffee into the car when you drive your children to school, your children will be much more likely to accept the "No food or drink in the car" rule. It's that simple. The consistency, continuity, and predictability with which you maintain everyday structure, rules, and boundaries creates the foundational set of overall values that remains intact in the face of the necessary exception. Life demands exceptions. They're inevitable. Parents get into trouble, not because of the exceptions, but because they fail to lay the everyday foundation that can withstand the exception.

Aha! You Didn't Take Us Seriously, Did You?

Here's that devilish old logic again. We're all brilliant at coming up with spur-of-the-moment rationalizations, and parents are no exception. So some of you who agree with what you just read will nonetheless come up with an instantaneous exception to the exception-to-the-rule rule today. All you have to do, in order to break the "No mundane exceptions" rule, is to come up with a perfectly logical-sounding reason why *this* exception ought to be allowed. Such second-order exceptions always do sound perfectly logical. In fact, within a very narrow context (perhaps just the sentence itself), such exceptions *are* logical. For example:

- Taking a five-year-old to a PG-13 movie on the grounds that "He can handle it."
- Taking a thirteen-year-old who gets into trouble for fighting

to a professional hockey game because he knows that "These are adults, not children, and they get paid for this stuff."

- Taking a third grader out of school for a four-day family vacation immediately after a four-day weekend on the grounds that "It's educational, and besides it's too dangerous to drive on holidays."

Parents don't go to PG-13 movies because their five-year-old "can handle it." Parents go to PG-13 movies because they want to, or because they don't want to see another hundred-million-dollar commercialized fairy tale. But even if he *could* "handle it," what else will the five-year-old decide to handle on his own as a result of this instance of rule-breaking?

When parents use rationalizations to break rules and violate boundaries, they are just as likely to use rationalizations to *create* rules and boundaries for the convenience of the moment. Thus, we often encounter situations like the following:

- Saying to a six-year-old, "These toys are only to look at. They're not to buy."
- Saying to an eight-year-old—who knows his mother sends him to a classroom where, much of the school year, a good quarter of the students have a cold—"We're not going to Grandma's house today because she's got a cold."

There is no question but that it takes considerable effort and a lot of concentration to maintain the kind of baseline consistency that helps to build the foundation of values and character that you want for your child. But, by taking these things seriously, you will be building much more than that. By not throwing wrenches into the works of your child's development, you will radically decrease the likelihood that he or she will develop those cognitive-behavioral styles that are routinely identified, diagnosed, labeled, miseducated, and mistreated today.

Boundaries and Bed-Sharing

When young children we are working with don't respond to what seems to be a genuine improvement in structure, rules, and boundaries at home, it is often a sign that one particular boundary has not been tightened—bed-sharing. Apart from the occasional brief jump into Mom and Dad's bed to cuddle before getting up, we discourage parents from sleeping with their children. As much as sleeping with young children may seem natural, it's dangerous and can even be fatal.

In a now-classic study that lasted from the mid-1970s to the mid-1980s and was published in the *Journal of Forensic Sciences* in 1978, James L. Luke, M.D., the chief medical examiner of the District of Columbia, found that over 50 percent of cases of sudden infant death syndrome (SIDS) occurred under conditions of bed-sharing. "Crib death" was clearly a misnomer. Luke found that the majority of SIDS cases involved babies sleeping with at least one adult. As he indicated in his article, there are no distinguishing differences between the gross and microscopic signs of subtle asphyxiation (as from rolling over on a baby) and those found in bona fide cases of babies who stop breathing without apparent cause.

As much as it may seem as natural for human parents, mothers especially, to sleep with their babies as for dogs or cats to sleep with their puppies and kittens, it's not at all the same. Four-legged mammals are built very differently than two-legged humans. Humans can roll over easily in both directions; dogs, cats, lions, and tigers can't. When pups and kittens are huddled in the soft, warm space created by the mother cat's legs and belly, they're actually protected. If mama cat is going to roll over, she'll go in the other direction. And, as far as we know, animal mothers don't have other things on their minds, don't cuddle with their mates when nursing, and certainly don't consume sedating substances like medications and alcohol. It's just not wise to sleep with babies.

Beyond that, bed-sharing blurs important physical, personal, and psychological boundaries. Separating, moving away from Mother is a natural part of development. Crawlers first do it when they venture away from Mom and then look back or crawl back occasionally to reestablish contact. Eventually, they wander off altogether. When this natural separation process is not allowed to take place, a *hostile-dependent* attachment can develop, an aggressive overattachment of child to mother. For example, a couple brought their 140-pound stocky fourth grader to see us because of oppositional-defiant behavior, a hostile-dependent relationship with his mother, and the fact that, no matter whether he went to bed in his own bed or on the couch, Bruce always ended up in bed with his parents or one of his three sisters. Bruce was constantly in everyone's space and into everyone's business.

Bruce had been an inconsolable colicky baby who could not be allowed to cry because of bilateral groin hernias that could not be surgically repaired until he was about two. (Crying hard is just like straining at stool. It raises the pressure in the abdomen—very dangerous when hernias allow the bowel to be pushed through passages that should be closed at birth.) And that's just what Bruce did all the time: cry. To make matters even worse, Bruce's reaction to traditional infant sedatives like Benadryl or phenobarbital was to get even more wired and to strain even harder as he cried. The only solution was for Mom and Dad to take turns staying up at night, rocking baby Bruce. Nine years later, when we first met him, Bruce was still in constant motion at night, and his entire family was both wired and exhausted.

The constant motion actually turned out to be the key to the solution to the nightly bed invasion that was driving Bruce's family up the wall. At our suggestion, Bruce's parents got him a waterbed, the baffleless kind that wiggles all over whenever you move your body. Once he could both sleep and be rocked at the same time, Bruce slept soundly in his own bed. With that, the constant forays into his family members' space subsided.

"But You Haven't Seen the Look of Abject Terror in Her Eyes!"

Bruce's case was unusual. Julie's case was much more typical. Seven-year-old Julie had been sleeping with her mom for two years by the time her mother came alone to ask for some advice. Julie was an adoptee, taken home from the hospital by her parents the day after she was born. When she was five, Julie's parents divorced. Her mother felt horrible for Julie. Not only had Julie been given away once, she had now lost another parent, a father who now had practically nothing to do with her. And, to make matters even more poignant, Julie's mom was an adoption counselor! Julie's mom felt as if she had failed doubly: not only had she not been able to keep her marriage together, she had failed to provide Julie with the perfect mom and dad she felt her daughter deserved.

Julie played her mother's guilt to the max. If her mother asked her to clean up her room, Julie would reply, "You can't tell me what to do! You're not my *real* mother!" If her mother showed even the slightest irritation at such nasty replies, Julie, sniffing out her mother's embarrassment and vulnerability like a seasoned hunting dog, would say, "You're yelling at me! This is child abuse! I'm calling nine-one-one!" "And, you know," her mother told us, "she would!"

In spite of her daughter's outright defiance and brilliantly timed threats, Joan found it very hard to see the manipulative nature of Julie's need to sleep with her. When Joan was told that Julie's nighttime fears were unrealistic, she exclaimed, "But you haven't seen the look of abject terror in her eyes!"

"Why?" Denis replied. "What have you got in there, Freddy Kruger?"

"No . . . ," Joan replied. "But she IS really scared. She's terrified."

There are few greater gifts that a parent can give her child than *comfort in her own space*. A child's own bed is the very essence of her own space, and being able to sleep comfortably there is the very essence of feeling safely comfortable in her own home.

The first thing Joan had to do was to get rid of her guilt. She was filling the responsibility vacuum left by the man and woman who had given Julie life and by Joan's ex-husband, who had decided that he preferred *not* being married and *not* being a father. In Julie's logical mind, if her mom was behaving as if she were guilty, then she *was* guilty—and deserved to be treated as such. So Joan had to stop feeling, and expressing, the sense of responsibility that no one else would own up to.

Since the only way Julie would ever learn that she was genuinely safe in her own bed would be *for her to experience that safety over and over*, Joan had to get Julie back there. After all, there were no Freddy Krugers, vampires, monsters, or other horrors in Julie's room to justify her terror.

"Be prepared," Joan was told, "not to get much sleep for the next three to four nights. It will be exhausting—but nothing compared to trying to get Julie out of your bed when she's twelve! Since the only way that Julie will know that you really believe it's safe for her to be in her own bed is for you to behave *as if you really believe it*, simply put her to bed as if she were going to stay there. Then, when she comes to your bed, you take her back—as many times as you have to. When you carry her or lead her back to her own bed, don't get angry, don't get upset, and don't repeat any nighttime rituals. After the first good-night kiss, that's it, no more. Be prepared to do this as many as forty times the first night. It'll taper off after that."

"But she'll sneak back in, and I won't know it until she bumps me and I wake up at three or four in the morning."

"That's fine. It doesn't matter. If that happens, just get up and take her back."

"And, by the way," Denis continued, "here's what you do about the rest. The next time you tell Julie to clean up her room and she tells you that you can't tell her what to do because you're not her 'real' mother, you say, 'I *am* your *real* mother. But, if you want to find that other lady who didn't want you, I'll be more than happy to help you find her—AFTER you clean up your room.' "

"You don't know my daughter!" Joan protested. "She'll take me up on that!"

"No she won't."

"Yes she will!"

"No. She won't. And when you tell Julie to empty the dishwasher and she yells, 'This is child abuse! I'm calling nine-one-one!' you say, 'Julie, I'll be more than happy to dial the number for you myself—AFTER you empty the dishwasher.' "

"Wow, you *really* don't know my daughter!" Joan protested again. "She knows we live in a very small community. She'll take me up on that, too!"

"No she won't. Give it a try. You'll see," Denis said.

The next week Denis was fully prepared to repeat his sales job on how to get Julie out of Joan's bed, but it wasn't necessary. Joan had actually done what Denis had recommended.

"It was amazing," Joan said. "I would never have believed it possible, but it worked. I had to get up about twenty times the first night, about eleven or twelve the next, and just three or four the third night. The fourth night, she actually stayed in her bed. And the fifth night, she even turned out the light."

"You mean that you two were sleeping with the light on for the last two years?"

"Yep." Joan smiled sheepishly. "I don't know why I risked it, but I even said what you told me to say when Julie wanted her 'real mother' and threatened to call nine-one-one. She did what I told her to do and hasn't even brought the subject up again since."

The Joan and Julie episode took place a good twenty years before this book was written. Since that time, and in the fifteen years that we have worked together, we have never seen it take over a week to get a child to sleep comfortably in his or her own bed, regardless of how long they had previously slept with a parent. In fact, we've never seen the process take more than four consecutive nights. What often *does* take a long time, however, is convincing the parent(s) that (1) this approach will work and (2) that they are not being horrible insensitive ogres for going ahead in the face of "abject terror" and protests that they "don't care" and are "mean and horrible." Even those parents who find the first few nights genuinely exhausting are quick to acknowledge that the brief struggle they've just been through was nothing compared to the thought of more years of trying to accomplish the task with verbal reassurances, upset, and frustration.

Once the child is back in his or her own bed (or in their own bed for the very first time), we typically see a decrease in oppositionalism, defiance, outright aggression, and hostile dependence. Parents then find it much easier to create new structures within the family, to enforce existing rules, and to maintain all sorts of boundaries. Once in his or her own bed, the child typically experiences a real sense of accomplishment. Enjoyable time in the child's bedroom increases during the day as well, which, in turn, decreases the child's previous demand for daytime closeness with busy parents.

It's important that parents be consistent and not give in later to protests that "This is different, there's a real storm!" and the like. Even in the case of genuinely scary experiences in which parents might give in and allow the child into bed with them (such as a break-in, a robbery in the neighborhood, or a tree falling on part of the house during a storm), it is important to get the child back into his own bed, his own safe space, as quickly as possible. That return to normalcy keeps the structure solid and the boundaries secure.

13

The Five Minutes: How to Make Sure That Your Child Will Talk to You Forever

Lots of parents tell us that their kids talk to them all the time. "My son has absolutely no trouble telling me exactly what's on *his* mind!" says a dad.

"You mean," we say, "that your son has no trouble being rude, disrespectful, oppositional, and defiant—that he's not afraid to tell you straight out?"

"No trouble at all!" says the dad. Yet when asked to tell us what *really substantive thoughts, fears, desires, or experiences* his son has shared with him lately, this dad, like so many parents, is hard-pressed to come up with a single example.

"When's the last time your son asked you why you never go to any of his sport activities? Or when's the last time your son said something like 'Dad, I think you're really scared of losing your job'? Or when's the last time your daughter told you that she knows you and your wife have been arguing and she's scared to death that the two of you are going to get a divorce?"

Even in homes where parents and children talk regularly, where families actually sit down to evening meals together, more is often left unsaid than ever gets communicated. Even in homes where parents are sensitive and tuned-in, small oversights, minor lapses of memory, momentarily hurt feelings, or busy schedules often convey the mistaken impression that parents don't *really* want to hear what's on their children's minds. And even the most caring and committed of parents are not without their own sensitivities and defensiveness—all of which can effectively say to a child "Don't tell me what you're really thinking."

"You Can Tell Me Anything"

The dad we just encountered assumes that what he hears on a daily basis is what's really on his son's mind. At this stage he makes no bones about the fact that it's hard for him to listen to his son because their relationship has already become chronically tense. Many parents, especially those with younger children, know that they've not yet reached the same level of tension and mutual enmity, but they're just as frustrated because their children aren't talking either. These parents are confused because, as many have told us over the years, they have repeatedly reassured their children that they were more than willing to listen. "Of course I'm interested in you," they've told their children. "You can tell me anything!"

Since they experience themselves as genuinely available, these parents are saddened and frustrated by the fact that their children don't seem to say anything of consequence to them. They feel left out, that they're not a part of their child's innermost experiences and feelings.

By now, you're probably realizing what's actually going on. This is our old "postal" version of communication—where parents mistakenly assume that, if they haven't received the message, it must not have been sent. Unfortunately, what these sincere and well-intentioned parents don't realize is that they have placed the burden of communication on the

child—often the very young child. *What these parents gave their children was permission to share, not the conviction that they were really there to listen.*

The Disappearance of Interest

Think back to when your child was a baby. Think of the times when you could literally lose yourself in contemplation, when her every movement was awe-inspiring and kept you glued to that little being for what must have seemed like eternities. Think back to how important it was to you that your baby look at you and how warm and fulfilled you felt when she seemed to drink in your very being through her gaze. Think of how you hung on her every babble and coo, listening intently for that first recognizable word, hoping it would be "mama." That was connectedness. Like being in love. How marvelous it must have been to be on the other side, soaking up your rapt attention!

Now ask yourself: When was the last time you looked at your child with that same rapt attention? When did you last hang on every word?

Unfortunately, it doesn't take very long for parents to begin to take children for granted. With the development of the child's autonomy, parental attention tends to shift away from *who the child is* to *what the child is doing*—doing "right" or doing "wrong." For many parents, paying attention to their child's productions—drawings, cut-outs, toy arrangements, etc.—gradually replaces paying attention to who they are. And whereas before, during those magic baby years, parents often broke from what they were doing to plunge themselves fully into rapt absorption, now they break from household chores or TV football games to cast a furtive glance or comment in passing on what's right or what's wrong, what's good or what's bad.

Wonderment shrinks, life becomes commonplace, and interest dwindles. Is it any wonder that children rarely talk to their parents?

Becoming Interested Again

Do you have to fall back in love with your child to convince him or her that you are genuinely there, genuinely tuned-in, and genuinely interested? No, and society's structure, rules, and boundaries tend to make that quite impractical anyway. Besides, that kind of intense connectedness wouldn't serve your child's growing needs for independence and autonomy. So, if the intensity's not necessary, what is? Do you have to set aside long periods of time to convince your child that you're genuinely tuned-in and genuinely interested? Fortunately, the answer is no.

It's actually quite easy to help your child grow up simply taking for granted that he or she can tell you anything and everything—and that you will always be there to listen with your full attention, your complete understanding, and your genuine empathy. Obviously, it's easiest to do if you're starting out at the beginning, but, even if your child is already eight, twelve, or sixteen and not talking to you, it's not too late. All that is required is patience, perseverance, and the willingness to put up with some initial frustration.

The Five Minutes

The Five Minutes is a simple yet highly structured and tightly boundaried communication technique designed to provide children and adolescents with a reliable ongoing experience of genuine parental interest in their feelings, experiences, opinions, and desires. The Five Minutes has a history that reflects our developing understanding and appreciation of the simple subtleties of parent-child relationships and communication.

We originally created the Five Minutes in response to the lives of the military families we were working with during the early 1980s. Because unpredictability and constant change—from training absences, scheduled deployments, and base reassignments to unexpected rapid mobilizations—are often the only "consistent" experience in the lives of military families, our only goal at first was to make sure these parents spent at least some "quality" time alone with each child every day. And since busy parents (not to mention single parents or those with many children) are always complaining that they have NO time, we made the time burden as short as possible—a mere five minutes. At least that way they couldn't justify not giving it a try on the grounds that "there just isn't enough time in the day."

Despite its minimal structure, our humble technique seemed to work. In some families, just the fact that kids could count on their private time alone with each parent every day resulted in increased stability and less disruption. We quickly discovered, however, that as we refined our understanding of children's experience, the logic of language, and the subtle realities of parent-child communication, we could also begin to refine both the Five Minutes itself and what we felt we could reasonably expect from it.

Genuine Communication Depends on More Than Just "Quality Time"

Most people tend to think of "quality time" as simply enjoyable time spent together—such as a family picnic or going to a soccer game with your thirteen-year-old. The Five Minutes is very different: you don't expect to hear earth-shattering revelations from your child or adolescent during "quality time" at an amusement park, but you do expect to hear personally meaningful things from your child during the Five Minutes.

The structure of the Five Minutes is deceptively simple.

- Five minutes a day alone, in private, with each child *every single day* except when absolutely impossible.
- The Five Minutes is not to be interrupted. No TV, radio, music, phone calls, beepers, little brothers barging in, or other disturbances of any kind.
- No other activities (games, play) will compete with the Five Minutes.
- No touching is allowed: no holding, rocking, back or foot rubbing.
- Although you may refer to them as "our" Five Minutes, it's the child's time to talk to you, not your time to talk to your child.
- During his or her Five Minutes, your child may tell you anything he or she cares to say—respectfully, of course.
- Your response is to understand and validate how your child feels about whatever is being expressed or recounted.

- Do NOT explain, excuse, or correct your child's version—even if he or she is factually wrong.

The Five Minutes Is Not a Gimmick or a Cure-All

The Five Minutes is a *process*, not a gimmick or a quick fix. Nor can the Five Minutes substitute for all those things you can do to improve parent-child communication and relationships that we've already discussed in the book. So remember that the Five Minutes doesn't take place in a vacuum. We trust that, by now, you're listening very carefully to your child during the course of the day; that your understanding of his or her experience has become much richer and more refined; that you're saying what you mean and meaning what you say; that you're dealing with the complexities of structure, rules, and boundaries and responsibility and choice with much greater sensitivity and consistency. However important, the Five Minutes is just one part of good strategic parenting.

In essence, the Five Minutes:

- Costs nothing, requires very little time and no paraphernalia
- Provides a thread of consistent and reliable experience
- Creates a calming, stabilizing effect over time
- Promotes honest, open, and trusting communication
- Helps build an honest, open, and trusting relationship
- Operationally defines the meaning of "commitment," "dependability," "care," "attention," "listening," and "understanding"

To be effective, the Five Minutes

- MUST be done on a regular basis over time
- MUST be done consistently according to the rules that structure it

It's that simple.

Introducing the Five Minutes

Tell your child that you're going to spend a *special Five Minutes* together each day, that it's their time to share with you whatever's on their mind, and that you are going to just be there and be a genuine listener. Tailor what you say according to your child's age and to how you've gotten along up to this point.

With young children, just announce that you're going to do the Five Minutes and then proceed to do so. You can define the structure, rules, and boundaries of the Five Minutes over time, just as we define the structure, rules, and boundaries of our therapeutic space operationally in our ongoing clinical work with each child and family. Detailed explanations are not needed.

With older children and teenagers, simply introduce the Five Minutes in a matter-of-fact manner, perhaps stressing how hectic life has been or your feeling that you've been missing out on some of what they've been experiencing in life.

On the other hand, if you know that you really *haven't* been a good listener, don't avoid the issue. Say something like "I know I've been distracted lately, so we're going to have a special time each day when you can tell me *anything*—and I'll be there one hundred percent to listen carefully to what you have to say." That defines exactly what the Five Minutes is about. It's also no longer the same old "You can tell me anything" because this time you're going to replace good intentions with real actions.

If your teenager replies, "What's this, another one of those touchy-feely ideas from those books you read?" don't get defensive. Just say, "No, it's part of our new relationship."

And if your older child or teenager says, "Gee, 'Da Five Minutes,' *that's* dumb," don't get defensive and try to "slip it in" without your teenager noticing by calling it something else or by not giving it a name at all. The name "The Five Minutes" is important. That "silly name" is actually a boundary: it defines the Five Minutes as unique and different than any other time you may spend talking or just being together. Names are important: you'll actually lose much of the power of this simple little technique to define and facilitate a unique relationship if you skip it or rename it. For once, we'll say, "Just trust us on this one." By now, we've actually been through this hundreds of times.

Rules and Boundaries Structuring the Five Minutes

The time together is to be private and uninterrupted. "Private" means that each parent should spend his or her time alone with each child. "Uninterrupted" means that literally, during those precious five minutes, you are not going to do anything or respond to anything that disrupts the process: you won't go to the bathroom, answer the phone, look at your beeper, or do anything other than to give 100 percent of your attention to your child.

Pick a place where you won't have to spend all of your time trying to deal with distractions. It's all right to use the child's bedroom, but, if you do, be careful not to make the Five Minutes into a nighttime ritual. You'll see why as we continue to explain the subtleties of the Five Minutes.

Apart from the obvious reason that every child deserves his or her own time with each parent, children also have unique relationships with each parent and rarely do they say the same things to both. It's also very difficult, if not impossible, for most children to share angry, hurt, or embarrassed feelings with one parent if the other is present.

Finally, parent by modeling: if you don't want your child to interrupt you when you're on the phone or talking to a neighbor, treat your child as if he or she deserves the same consideration for their Five Minutes.

The Five Minutes should take place every day. If we haven't already convinced you of the importance of consistency, continuity, and pre-dictability, just ask yourself what your child's reaction might be if you started the process and then stopped it abruptly: *"You mean I'm not even worth five minutes!?!"* As brief as this minuscule amount of time may be, it represents a commitment and an attitude of openness, acceptance, and *interest* whose full impact is not felt until it is withdrawn.

Look at it this way: a single brick is insignificant—but if you patiently place brick after brick, brick upon brick, you can build gigantic buildings.

It's not the amount of time spent daily that gives the Five Minutes its power, it's the fact that you do it day after day, month after month, year after year. It's the consistency and continuity over time that conveys to your child the absolute genuineness of your interest and concern. It's the fact that, time after time, you listen patiently that conveys to your child that you really do care, and that he or she can really tell you anything.

Sometimes, of course, interruptions are inevitable. So if circumstances really do make you miss the Five Minutes three days in a row, should you do fifteen minutes to make up? No, you just pick up where you left off and try to maintain the continuity as best you can. If the next Five Minutes just happens to develop into a longer meaningful moment, that's fine. But no extra time is required.

Parents who have to be away from home—staying late at the office, being at a meeting, or being out of town—can do the Five Minutes by phone. Be sure that you separate it from the rest of your conversation (talking about the soccer game, the prom, the fun your child had on a school outing) by saying something like "Okay, let's do our Five Minutes now." We've worked with many families who have maintained a real and satisfying sense of being connected through their "phone Five Minutes."

The Five Minutes is not to compete with any other activity. Don't expect anything significant to happen while all the trappings of daily life are invading your private space—things like television, radio, video games, wild computer screen savers, chess, and checkers.

This also means that you can't do the Five Minutes while traveling together in a car or while doing a household chore. If you're doing *any-thing* else, you're not doing the Five Minutes. So, even if you've just had the most intimate and revealing forty-minute discussion with your child or teenager on the drive home from school, *don't skip the Five Minutes that day.* If you do, count on your child's logical response: "That's great. I open up and talk to you once and what do you do? You skip the Five Minutes!"

If, on the other hand, you happen to be traveling, you don't have to postpone the Five Minutes until you're back in your own space. In fact, *under such circumstances only,* you can do the Five Minutes practically anywhere, even in an airplane or airport waiting lounge. Just find a place that's as private as possible.

Many children, younger children especially, want to play games during their "special time." Just explain that there's lots of time to play together but that this is your special Five Minutes for talking and sharing feelings. Don't get put off or feel that the process is not working if your child says, "Well, then I'm not talking!" Just say something like "Sure you are! You're talking to me right now, so tell me how you felt when . . ." and refer back to something that you know was meaningful to your child. If you child is stubborn and persists in not talking, don't worry. This is a process. It will come.

No touching is allowed during the Five Minutes. Would you reveal your innermost thoughts to someone rubbing your feet? Are you kidding! If you're rubbing your child's back during the Five Minutes, you've been snookered into being an unpaid masseuse at a most inappropriate moment. So don't count on your child sharing anything significant, especially anything that could be painful or upsetting to you, if you're touching, rubbing, scratching. Touching can be a very subtle way of saying "I'm so close to you that you couldn't possibly get upset at me, could you?" You will find that the content of the Five Minutes will be much richer if you stay in your space and your child stays in his or her space. Yes, you can sit on your child's bed—if you have no other place to sit—but make sure that you're positioned so that it's clear that you're having your Five Minutes and not a bedtime tête-à-tête.

Our rule is a serious one, but it's not absolute. Of course you can touch and console your child if he or she shares something very painful or traumatic. In fact, many parents have told us that the Five Minutes allowed them to learn about past hurts they would never have imagined. But even if something unexpected does come up, move slowly because there may be even more yet to come. If you rush too quickly to console your child, you may not hear the rest. If, on the other hand, your child is a crier and a toucher, be a stickler on the "No touching" rule.

The Five Minutes is the child's time to talk to the parent, not vice versa. We're the first to admit that this relationship is absolutely unfair and unbalanced. Fairness means "an equal part to each," and, in this case, it's the child who needs to feel understood and accepted by the parent, not vice versa. At first, some parents feel that at last their child has become a captive listener—but that's NOT what the Five Minutes is all about.

Some parents also feel uncomfortable with silence, so they talk or ask questions to fill up the time. Resist this urge! *If you don't, your child won't talk to you*—there just won't be any free time. And besides, whether you intend to or not, filling up the quiet time communicates to your child that you're uncomfortable with both the process and with whatever he or she might say. This, of course, decreases the likelihood that your child will ever open up to you. If you are uncomfortable, just treat the Five Minutes as an exercise in patience and in becoming comfortable with silence.

Don't worry that nothing is happening during silence, because the time is neither lost nor wasted. The silence is misleading because most children beyond the toddler years are thinking quite actively while not saying a word—*they're talking to you in their minds*. Once children discover that their thoughts don't make you angry, drive you away, or cause you to give up on them, they'll start to talk openly.

A few children, however, may take weeks or even months before they open up. While these children are in the minority, it can be very frustrating if the holdout happens to be your child. If that's the case, *don't give up* and *don't give in* to the urge to fill up the silence. Just consider it the path that must be taken to open communication. Children who take a long time to start talking are either extraordinarily stubborn—in which case sticking with the process is your only creative alternative—or they're really worried or scared about what's on their minds or about your potential reaction.

In this case as well, just as only the experience of staying in their own bed can convince children that it's safe to go to bed alone, only the experience of your not fleeing or abandoning the process will convince these children that it's safe to begin to share what's on their mind. Remember that giving up on a child who's not talking will feel like you're *giving up on them*. Since silent children haven't yet said anything that could drive you away, you must be reacting to *who they are* and not just to their words. Remember that being there every single day communicates how important your child is to you more powerfully than words could ever do.

Finally, keep in mind that even children who seem oblivious register much more than people think. If a parent wants out of a relationship like the Five Minutes, the child can provide that easy out simply by not talking. When that happens, both child and parent lose.

Your child can tell you anything during the Five Minutes— respectfully, of course. Contrary to the initial reaction of some parents, we're not ganging up on you. The Five Minutes is not a time for your child to read you the riot act or to be disrespectful but to share with you what they normally never share. Anger is also acceptable—again, provided that it is expressed respectfully. All you need to do is to let your child know that you really do understand how they feel. The Five Minutes is NOT, however, a means by which your child can get you to abandon personal and family values or rules.

Do NOT explain, excuse, or correct your child's version—even if he or she is factually wrong. We hope that by now the rationale for this rule is clear to you. When you explain, excuse, or correct, what the logical mind of the child or adolescent hears is "You're wrong"—wrong to think what she thinks and feel what she feels.

Explanations: When your five-year-old complains that you didn't save him a piece of pie, resist that urge to remind him that you asked him twice if he wanted some before you gave the remaining sliver to his younger brother. Just tell him, "Yes, it's sad that you didn't get any. Sure, I can understand that you're really upset."

Excuses: When your teenager starts to boil and says, "My father lied to me again! He promised he'd come to at least one game, and now he's missed the last one of the season!" don't tell him that his dad got tied up at work—whether true or not. Your teenager will still take it personally, and he'll feel like slime for being so mad at a parent who had such a good excuse.

Wrong versions: Even if your child or teenager has it completely wrong, don't say "But that's not how it happened" or "But that's not what I meant" because, once again, the essence of what you're saying is "You're wrong." And that's usually all the child or adolescent will hear.

It's hard for all of us not to explain, excuse, or clarify perspectives because not doing so makes us feel as if we're agreeing with what the other person is *saying*, rather than validating how the other person is *feeling*.

We had a poignant illustration of how powerful the Five Minutes can be in the case of a fourteen-year-old who had been hit by a car when he was four. Because he was initially unconscious for months, his doctors thought he would never get out of bed, let alone walk again. By the time we met him, ten years had passed and he had progressed from bed to wheelchair to under-arm crutches and finally to the arm-grip variety. Bert was left palsied, with rag-doll coordination and garbled speech. In the process, he had lost his father, a super-macho sports addict who had no interest in being around a son who couldn't control his drooling, let alone play contact sports.

Bert's abysmal self-esteem was reflected in his poor attention to personal hygiene and lack of care for his own things. His constant passive-aggressiveness reflected an all-pervasive anger that he smilingly denied. He ridiculed his stepfather and was constantly mean and disrespectful to his mother. Yet for years Bert had denied any anger over the accident. In fact, Bert was never "angry," yet we met him because he had just microwaved the family cat!

One day, in the middle of the Five Minutes and without any warning, Bert became red in the face and screamed at his mother, "Where in the hell were *you* when I got hit?" Fortunately, Bert's mother understood the purpose of the Five Minutes and the reasons for our three rules. As shocked as she was, and as much as it hurt, she didn't blurt out what she so badly wanted to say. Bert's mom could have explained truthfully that she was on the other side of town, buying groceries, so there was no way in the world she could have saved her son. And she could have further excused herself by pointing out—again, truthfully—that Bert's father, who was supposed to be looking after him, chose to lie down and take a nap, thereby allowing his four-year-old son to ride his Big Wheel into the rush-hour traffic.

So when the explosion finally came, Bert's mother understood it for what it was—and let him know how much she *did* understand his sense of abandonment. Without explanations or excuses, but with tears streaming down her cheeks, Bert's mom said simply, "You must have felt *terribly* abandoned by me!"

Within days of his outburst during the Five Minutes with his mother, Bert's personal hygiene improved and his constant passive-aggressiveness eased considerably. What was even more amazing, however, was the fact that Bert stopped soiling his underwear—something he had done daily since the accident. Bert's soiling was something over which he was supposed to have no control—the result of brain damage.

Not every family has such potent issues hidden beneath the surface, but Bert's story does show the immense power of open and direct communication for creating change.

(For answers to at least some of the many questions this chapter may have raised, see the appendix "Parents Ask About the Five Minutes" following chapter 15.)

14

Zero to Three, Bad Genes,
and "Normal" Development:
How Much Do Parents
Have to Worry?

What we've said so far does make sense, doesn't it? We've offered you a view of children and parent-child relations that is absolutely new—and yet so accessible to everyday observation that anyone can validate it by simply taking the time to watch, listen, and think.

We've shown you that many of the perplexing problems that parents encounter daily are actually due to avoidable miscommunication and to a simple failure to understand children on their own terms. We've shown you as well that simply by minimizing miscommunication and by beginning to appreciate the complexity and subtlety of even the youngest children, you can use that new understanding to avoid the pitfalls of dead-end educational and psychiatric labeling, miseducation, and mistreatment.

But we also know from years of experience that, even when they learn to validate these things on their own, and even when they're able to solve many of the problems that previously made them want to opt out of parenthood, parents start second-guessing themselves again. As if that weren't enough, we've also found that the constant barrage of new findings, new theories, new technology, and ever-changing expert opinions that fill the media often begin to eat away at parents' newfound knowledge and self-assurance. So, to help counter this understandable tendency to slip back into self-doubt and second-guessing, we're going to look briefly at just a few issues that tend to undermine parents' confidence.

Should You Worry About Zero to Three and "Missed Windows of Opportunity"?

If anything's important, it's the foundation upon which your child's life is built, and, obviously, you should do everything you can to make sure that it is solid and healthy. But what if your child is already four or fourteen and you begin to hear that the first three years of life are absolutely crucial, that the next seven are extremely important, and that the brain's most important wiring is completed during those first vital years? Should you worry? After all, many experts are saying that after three (or ten), it's all over. So how concerned should you be that you may have failed to provide your child with the right kind and the right amount of experience in those early "crucial" years?

The answer is: Don't worry at all—it won't do you any good. The past is past but the present is full of opportunity. Besides, as William Greenough of the University of Illinois and the Beckman Institute and one of the world's foremost brain researchers once said to us, "Your brain isn't the same now as it was five minutes ago." Brain plasticity is part of life. You need to worry *only* if your child is prevented from seeing, hearing, and touching or is deprived of social experience including spoken or signed language very early in life. Otherwise, your child's brain will remain capable of reorganizing itself in response to meaningful experience for as long as your child lives. Let's see why.

William Greenough and his colleague James Black, also at the University of Illinois at Urbana-Champaign and the Beckman Institute, distinguish between two types of brain plasticity. The first, most fundamental kind seems to "count on" certain categories of sensory experience such as light, sound, and touch—the basic sensory modalities that allow us to know the physical structure of the world. Over millions and millions of years, evolution has shaped the brain to "expect" certain fundamental sensory experience from the very beginning of life. Even with properly working eyes and ears, those parts of your child's brain that process visual and auditory input won't build the circuits necessary to work properly unless they are stimulated by the "expected" sensory input. Without that early stimulation, your child wouldn't be able to make useful sense of what she hears and sees. This is why a first language has to be learned during the very early years while the brain is in the process of massive circuit building and shaping.

The good news, however, is that for nearly everything else, the brain counts on another kind of brain plasticity that is capable of coping with new and changing circumstances. This kind of brain plasticity doesn't "expect" very specific categories of experience; instead, it "depends" upon changing and unpredictable experience to drive neural organization. This is the kind of brain plasticity necessary for learning about and dealing with the world on a daily basis. Because your child has to be able to adapt to an ever-changing world for as long as he or she lives, this kind of brain plasticity is "experience-dependent," and it will remain operational throughout your child's lifespan.

So don't worry if you didn't play Mozart recordings when your child was a baby! The door isn't closed and the circuits aren't all hard-wired. Besides, we already know from everything we've discussed earlier in the book that children respond to *meaning*, not just sounds. So, at any point in your child's life, if you want classical music—or any other kind of music, for that matter—to have the opportunity to play some kind of formative role, you will need to make it *meaningful* by sharing it, discussing it, or enjoying it together. Otherwise, simply playing Mozart or Frank Zappa won't shape your child's brain in any positive sense.

Now, why would music promote the sort of brain development that *might* aid other aspects of thinking? Because music is pure pattern—rhythmic and tonal pattern. Most people are at least minimally sensitive to the patterns that make up music, and, most of the time, you can increase that sensitivity by increasing the meaningfulness. The lesson of the so-called Mozart effect is not so much about music as it is about meaningful patterned experience, and this kind of experience is with us throughout life.

That's why it's important that you take advantage of the ability of your child's brain to respond to meaning NOW. But you don't have to go out and research the effects of classical music on the developing brain to do so. Just think back to the role of meaning in shaping children's attentional styles that we discussed in chapters 6, 7, and 8. You'll see that daily life offers you many opportunities to create meaningful patterned experience. That's why you can begin creating an organized brain or a disorganized brain through your own communication and interactive styles right from the beginning of your child's life. Or you can *change* your child's present attentional style by how you communicate and relate—even if your child is twelve or sixteen.

The lesson here is that your child's potential can be actualized only through meaningful experience. Notice that it doesn't matter whether experience is positive or negative, creative or destructive. If you skip the structure, rules, and boundaries that we discussed in chapter 12 and don't bother to put consistency, continuity, and predictability into your child's experience, you'll be shaping one kind of brain. If, on the other hand, you act on your understanding of the importance of structure for healthy development, you'll be shaping another kind of brain. If you continue to use ineffective and dissociogenic everyday communication styles, then you'll promote the development of an "ADD-style" brain. If, on the other hand, you really say what you mean and mean exactly what you say, you'll be providing the experiential input that favors organized attentional and cognitive styles. Every time you succeed in modifying any aspect of your child's cognitive-behavioral style by the way you communicate, structure experience, and convey support and understanding, you're playing a positive role in providing the experience that your child's brain utilizes to reorganize itself. Since evolution equipped your child with an experience-responsive brain, you may as well capitalize on that fact by utilizing its potential.

What About "Normal" Development?

Open any child psychology, psychiatry, or education textbook and you'll find chapters on normal development complete with tables of normal developmental milestones. What if your child is late in talking or walking or in developing fine motor control? Should you worry? If your baby shows absolutely no interest in the environment, then yes, it's time to consult your pediatrician. Or if your baby doesn't even crawl at one year

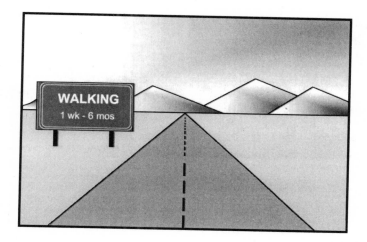

of age. But these are extreme examples. Most of the time, parents don't need to worry for the simple reason that *there is no one "right" or "correct" schedule of development.*

Esther Thelen and her colleagues Barbara Ulrich and Linda B. Smith have taken a fresh look at child development from a complex adaptive systems perspective. Because they have a special interest in motor development, they have done extensive research on how infants move from crawling to walking. What they found teaches us a lot about development in general.

The traditional view is to envision the acquisition of a developmental skill in terms of a pathway and to measure the child's progress in terms

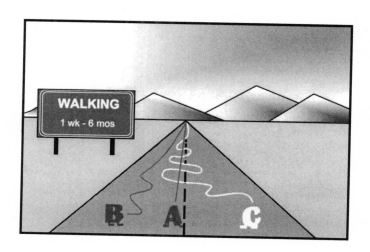

of milestones along that pathway. A child who progresses straight toward the goal and who gets there on time is viewed as "normal," while the child who does it differently or who takes longer would be viewed as having abnormal development. The longer the time taken or the more atypical the specifics of the child's development, the more "abnormal" it is.

Suppose you told people that the road in this second illustration represents the developmental pathway from crawling to walking and that the lines marked A, B, C represent the various developmental trajectories and then asked them to identify the child whose development was "normal." Which one do you think they would pick? And which one would they identify as "grossly abnormal"? Unless they suspect that you're asking them a trick question, you know what the answers will be—A will be "normal" and C will be "grossly abnormal."

This is not just an academic exercise because, in general, the education and mental health establishments really do believe that there is a "right" way to develop. This "right development" notion is reflected in crystallized form in the following graphic version of an ad for a now-classic book that appeared on a page of *Psychological Science*, a publication of the American Psychological Society.

Children are routinely assigned to programs or judged to be capable or incapable of using various educational or treatment modalities on the basis of where they are "developmentally." Every year children who deviate from that supposedly straight developmental pathway are shunted

---

Now in paperback...

STRAIGHT AND DEVIANT PATHWAYS FROM CHILDHOOD TO ADULTHOOD

Edited by Lee N. Robins and Michael Rutter

Presents longitudinal studies in psychopathology, extending from childhood into adulthood that address how personality and behavior predict adult outcomes.

into dead-end "special" educational programs and equally dead-end life-long psychiatric treatment regimens.

Now imagine how the folks on the street would respond to your questions using these terms. A would be on the "straight" pathway while C would clearly be the candidate for "deviant" development since his trajectory wandered all over the place.

Yet nothing could be farther from the truth, because there is no "correct" trajectory for any given aspect of development. Thelen and her colleagues discovered that if you actually pay attention to real children and don't remove all the unique features of their individual development through statistical smoothing, *no two children follow the same developmental trajectory.* And it doesn't matter whether you study two, twenty, two hundred, or two thousand children, no two will develop in the same way and at the same rate. So, even though C wandered all over the developmental pathway, by the time he got to his destination—walking—he looked no different than A, who supposedly "did it right." All individual development is unique. If you want to look at "normal" development, you have to remove everything that's unique from your data.

Thelen and her colleagues discovered another fascinating characteristic of children's development that didn't fit the standard developmental model—but that does fit what is known about the behavior of complex nonlinear dynamic systems. (This is the same "chaos theory" that Ian Malcolm used in *Jurassic Park* to explain why cloning dinosaurs was a very unpredictable and risky business.) Complex dynamic systems tend to stay in "preferred" states called *attractor states.* Attractor states are relatively stable. But, in order for a system to reorganize, it has to disintegrate—i.e., loosen up a bit—before new structures can be assembled. For example, a sleeping baby is in one attractor state, but when it wakes up, it moves into another attractor state where it will remain until it drifts off again. The transition from one relatively stable attractor state to another is called a *phase transition.* (You've recognized a phase transition whenever you've caught yourself nodding off.) Both development in general and specific behaviors are characterized by relatively stable attractor states that are punctuated by phase transitions, some of which are long and some of which are so brief that they may not even be noticed.

What Thelen and her colleagues found was that each time an infant was about to move from one level of motor competence to a new "higher" level on the pathway from crawling to walking, the infant's behavior became unstable. It got "worse." One might say that the stable structure of the infant's motor performance began to break up, to disaggregate until it completely disintegrated—only to reorganize into a new form. This is no news to anyone who has ever learned how to ride a bicycle. Rarely does one transit with elegant smoothness from the artificially maintained stability provided by training wheels to the self-supplied stability of balancing comfortably on two wheels. Instead, most of us go through a period of shakiness. That shakiness is the instability of the phase transition between being unable to stay up without crashing and what we routinely think of as bicycle riding.

Now, if there's anything Americans can't stand, it's unpredictability and instability. So imagine what would happen if a parent, teacher, or clinician mistook the instability necessary for adaptive change for disorder or dysfunction. We all know what would happen—they would probably try to "fix" the instability by suppressing it or by pushing the system back to a previous stable state. In dynamic systems terms, the process of preventing a phase transition is called *damping the system.*

And this is exactly what much parenting, education, and mental health treatment does. Whatever else they may do, most psychiatric drugs simply damp the system—they artificially lock the system into a particular attractor state. (When someone refers to a child on medication as "zonked," they're describing a damped system that is incapable of responding adaptively and creatively to a changing environment.) And while medications like stimulants may get rid of the troubling instability, damping agents also prevent the system from reorganizing. Thus, when the system "fails" to reorganize and move to what tends to be viewed as a more desirable stable state, parents, teachers, and clinicians mistakenly conclude that the system is "damaged" and assume that its "stuckness" is proof of its "inherent inability to change."

The disorder of instability *par excellence*, of course, is ADHD. Children who get saddled with this label are typically treated with Ritalin. Ritalin is the prince of system-damping medications. Stimulants like Ritalin, Dexedrine, Adderall, methamphetamine, and Cylert damp the transitional-transformational capacity of the child, which, of course, delights parents, teachers, and clinicians because the child is no longer annoyingly disruptive. By damping the system, stimulants simply make children's behavior more acceptable—*but that's all stimulants do*. Stimulants have no positive effect on cognition, learning, academic performance, or academic achievement that lasts beyond a matter of weeks. Thus the very system-damping effect of stimulants that makes children's obnoxious behavior less exhausting for adults creates the appearance of a lifelong "brain disorder" that can't be eliminated even with the "correct" medication.

The world is full of bright, creative people whose childhoods were characterized by abnormal—sometimes grossly abnormal—development. Nobel laureate Richard Feynman didn't talk until two and a half and even as an adult couldn't tell his right from his left. What's important is the overall process—not the hour-to-hour, month-to-month timetable followed by any child's development. However your child develops, your challenge is to maximize his or her potential.

Development Doesn't Require Micromanagement

The period from birth to three doesn't have to seem like a developmental minefield that parents can't cross without blowing something up, nor does development have to seem like a standardized test at which many normal children fail. Because children are complex adaptive *self-organizing* systems, it's simply not necessary for adults to micromanage development. So stop worrying about "normal" development. And don't assign negative, pathological meanings to the instability that is necessary for all adaptive change.

Think back to everything we covered in the first thirteen chapters. Most of the material was designed to help parents better understand their own children and to realize how many problems develop unnecessarily from everyday misunderstanding and miscommunication. By now it should be apparent why interference with intrinsically self-organizing processes is not necessary. Parenting and teaching are, first and foremost, a process of protecting and facilitating children's inherent potential for learning, growth, adaptation, health, and change. Again, that's why it's impossible to overstress that *what parents need to know about children* is the fundamental foundation upon which expert knowledge and expert intervention should be based—not vice versa. None of the developmental norms routinely applied to children by educational and mental health

professionals was developed based on a fundamental, realistic understanding of childhood cognitive-behavioral, communicative, attentional,
and affiliative styles that every parent can come to know.

Since Your Children Share the
Same Environment, Any Differences Among
Them Must Be Due to
Genetic Factors, Right?

Wrong. This is the myth of the shared environment. No two children
share the same environment—not even identical twins. In fact, the
womb can be such an inhospitable place for one twin that British pediatrician, researcher, and expert on twins Dr. Elizabeth M. Bryan notes that
it's not at all uncommon to discover the remains of a fetus "compressed
and embedded in the placenta of a healthy single baby." In these cases,
Bryan notes, the mother is usually unaware that she was ever carrying a
twin pregnancy. In other cases, no one will ever be aware that a twin was
lost because fetal deaths in the first trimester usually result in the resorp-
tion of the lost twin. About twice as many twins are stillborn as singletons, which means that it's possible that any of us may have once been a
twin. And even when both twins survive their intrauterine voyage in
good health, there is still the delivery to contend with, and exiting that
marvelous life vehicle presents a different challenge for each twin.

High-school physics reminds us that two bodies cannot occupy the
same space at the same time. This may seem awfully picky, but there's
really a very important lesson here, because it's not just that no two people can occupy the same physical space, but that no two people can
occupy the same *psychological* or *experiential* space.

To see how strikingly true this apparently self-evident statement
is, imagine two sisters—one the genetic offspring of two parents and
the other adopted. We know the two sisters can't share the same genetic
information because they're not related. But do they share the same
environment? When we take the actual experience of real children seriously, we discover that one sister has known with certainty who her par-

ents are, what they look like, and how they behave ever since she came into the world. The other was told that her "biological mother" gave her up for adoption because of circumstances in her life. So now one sister has one mother and the other has two mothers. One sister has lived through parental misfortune and ill health with the certainty of her parents' commitment to her, while the other was told that her "biological mother" gave her away precisely because of misfortune or ill health. Both sisters have always been told by their parents that they loved them, but one was also told that her biological mother "loved her so much that she gave her up for adoption." Both sisters have grown up in a family that kept their biological child, but one sister was told that she was given away because her biological mother "wanted her to have a family." No mention was ever made of the biological father. Finally, the older sister was four when her younger sister was adopted—which means that the two sisters were ten and six when their mother fell deathly ill and was confined to bed.

Now here's the question: What do *mother, father, family, love, care, commitment, belonging, misfortune,* and *loss* mean to these two sisters? We're not talking about words here—we're talking about concepts and actual subjective personal experiences. So, in very real experiential terms, does each sister have *a mother?* Does each sister have *the same mother?* Does each sister have *a father?* Does each sister *belong* to the *same family?* Has each sister experienced the *same maternal love?* Has each sister experienced the *same parental care?* Has each sister experienced the *same maternal commitment?* Has each sister experienced the *same misfortune and loss?* And, finally, had their mother actually died from her serious illness, would each sister have experienced the *same loss of a mother?*

The answer to all these questions is no. Every single aspect of these two girls' environment has a different meaning for them—and it is meaning, remember, that drives brain plasticity. So does it make any sense whatsoever to expect that these two radically different experiential-psychological environments should have the same effect on each sister? Again, the answer is no.

As we saw in chapter 4, children really do live in a very different world than adults imagine. And, unfortunately, the complexity, subtlety, and sophistication of children's experience is all but unknown to the general child-studies world, so it's not surprising that it has no impact upon the highly abstract, statistically based sub-sub-specialty of behavioral genetics. So, once again, take your child's—or each of your children's—individual worlds seriously. Only by doing so will you be able to meet their highly individual needs.

What About "Chemical Imbalances" and "No-Fault Brain Disorders"?

Many parents come to us convinced that their child suffers from a "chemical imbalance." Often they've been told that this is the case by physicians or mental health workers—sometimes after consultations that lasted only a matter of minutes. And even when we've been able to help children make radical changes in their behavior, academic performance, or relationships, worried parents will still often say, "Yes, but don't you think there could still be a chemical imbalance?" So before you start taking all of this too seriously, let's look at the reasoning behind the notion that chemical imbalances underlie all these child behavior problems.

"We know that children with psychiatric disorders have a chemical imbalance in the brain that is caused by a genetic abnormality," writes Harold S. Koplewicz, M.D., in *It's Nobody's Fault: New Hope and Help for Difficult Children and Their Parents*. But no sooner does he assure parents about the cause of childhood psychiatric disorders than Koplewicz hastens to add, "but we don't know what the specific abnormality is." This sounds more like faith than science. And the reasoning has a curiously familiar ring to it:

Children who meet standard criteria for a psychiatric disorder have a psychiatric disorder,

and

"We know that children with psychiatric disorders have a chemical imbalance in the brain that is caused by a genetic abnormality"

therefore

Children with standard psychiatric disorders have a chemical imbalance in the brain that is caused by a genetic abnormality.

By now this should sound extremely familiar! This is the same perfectly logical and meaningful circular reasoning that kids use to get you on technicalities—even when they're completely wrong. It's the same sort of reasoning that makes it possible to say "I have a headache. I take two aspirin and my headache goes away. Therefore, my headache was caused by aspirin deficiency." Good logic, bad thinking.

It's important to remember that thinking isn't divided into common folks' thinking, on the one hand, and scientific, professional, and expert thinking on the other. There is simply good thinking and bad thinking. Unfortunately, neither higher education nor professional specialty training immunizes against bad thinking. In fact, in some ways specialty training encourages bad thinking by creating the impression that the learner is acquiring "the latest," "the most sophisticated," or "the most specialized" knowledge. Rarely are students, at any level of education, routinely encouraged to challenge authority, to question their teachers or supervisors—in a word, to make uncertainty, skepticism, and hard-nosed criticism their primary learning mode. One typically pursues specialty training to know what the experts know, not to challenge them. So instead of the essential skepticism that makes for balanced and healthy learning, specialty training tends to confer authority, expertise, and CER-TAINTY. Parents don't need such certainty: they need real solutions to real problems.

Yet, as of this writing, there is not a single valid and reliable labora-tory test that can be used to diagnose psychiatric conditions, making psy-chiatry a minority of one among the medical specialties. This means that, traditionally, parents have had to depend upon the experts to explain the meaning of their child's problem behaviors since they can't get a lab test that will provide objective evidence of a psychiatric disorder. So, if you don't want to get lost in a closed loop of empty logic, don't go looking for the "chemical imbalances" caused by Koplewicz's "No-Fault Brain Disor-ders due to DNA-Roulette" (his words, not ours) which do NOT lead to "new hope and help for difficult children and their parents." All you'll find is categorical treatments for categorical disorders.

Ironically, the more sophisticated the diagnosing experts become, the more the Four D's (Disease, Disorder, Dysfunction, and Disability) come to predominate. Diagnosing Koplewicz's "No-Fault Brain Disorders due to DNA-Roulette" doesn't lead to solutions; it leads to the need for resignation, acceptance, and the willingness to live with the lifelong results of having a child with a genetically based "brain difference."

So, before you accept anyone's assertion that your child has a "No-Fault Brain Disorder" or a "chemical imbalance," look for simple commonsense explanations based on a realistic understanding of your child and the unique circumstances of his or her life—and then use the approaches that we've outlined to solve your problem.

The "ADHD Brain"—Myth or Reality?

"All that makes perfect sense," parents have told us, "but we've seen proof that these disorders are real." Below is surely what has become one of the icons of our present age—a positron emission scan showing a "normal" brain and an "ADHD brain" published by Alan Zametkin and his team at the National Institute of Mental Health. The 1990 *New England Journal of Medicine* article in which the illustration originally appeared has been routinely quoted in everything from the American Academy of Child and Adolescent Psychiatry's "Practice Parameters for the Assessment and Treatment of Children and Adolescents with Attention-Deficit/Hyperactivity Disorder" to hundreds of pop-psychology books.

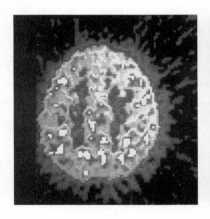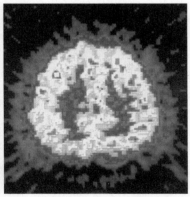

The image itself is a favorite of support groups, television, and the print media.

Which image, you may be wondering, represents the "normal" brain and which represents the "ADHD brain"? *It simply doesn't matter because no one has ever been able to replicate Zametkin's findings.* Worse yet, the article's conclusions aren't even supported by the data the article presents.

Let's look at a bit of history. Originally Lou, Henriksen, and Bruhn reported in the *Archives of Neurology* that 100 percent of eleven children diagnosed with ADHD had decreased blood flow in the frontal lobes and that 70 percent had decreased blood flow, as compared to their siblings, in a part of the brain that deals with attention, memory, and emotion called the caudate nucleus. Ritalin was said to increase metabolism in the caudate. Then, in 1989, the same research group found *no differences between an ADHD group and controls in any of the frontal lobe measures.* They reported inconsistent findings in another part of the brain, the right striatum, but not in the left.

So what should parents, teachers, and clinicians conclude when ADHD experts like John Hallowell and Russell Barkley cite the first findings of the Lou-Henriksen group and choose not to point out that the very same group failed to replicate them? Or when they fail to point out that, in the second set of experiments, there was no difference in performance on the vigilance task, clearly showing that there was *no attention deficit* in the ADHD group? In her long literature review "Ritalin and the Cocaine Connection," Diane McGuinness, professor emeritus of psychology at the University of South Florida, points out that when Zametkin and his colleagues attempted a follow-up study on seven of the original subjects, the only consistent effect of Ritalin was to *lower* glucose metabolism in all eight basal ganglia sites in the subjects' brains—results that were the very opposite of those reported by the Lou-Henriksen team in 1984. As McGuinness comments dryly, "It is clear that when proper data analysis is employed, no group differences can be found. In view of these highly inconsistent results, it is difficult to understand why these studies have made such an impact."

The failure of various researchers to replicate the findings that are routinely cited as "proof" of the biological nature of ADHD is not a collection of isolated instances. On the contrary, replication failures are very common. In fact, as Dr. Elliot Gershon of the National Institute of Mental Health is quoted as saying in a 1989 *Psychiatric Times* article entitled "Confidence Wanes in Search for Genetic Origins of Mental Illness," "The major problem is all the non-replications." Far from being a minor problem, the article refers to an "epidemic of non-confirmation," noting that researchers can't even agree on which portion of the chromosome is supposed to be the location for various guilty genes. So far, the article concludes, "the evidence is so equivocal that some competent observers deny that there is any convincing evidence for the genetic basis of any major psychiatric illness."

So, once again, if you want to actually solve your child's problems, you would be far wiser to forget about all the new findings and fancy technology and return to the basics of a realistic understanding of parent-child communication issues and how and why children behave and experience the world. THAT is where the vast majority of solutions lie.

15

A Reminder for Teachers
and Clinicians

Professionals who work with children face the very same challenges that parents do, simply because these challenges are the unavoidable consequences of being human. We all use language as a tool without realizing that language shapes us. We all behave as if conventional meaning were obvious to one and all. And we all tend to assume that others understand what we intend—whether or not our words and actions correspond to our intentions.

Whether they're parents or not, adults are so far removed from their own childhood that it literally requires a kind of anthropological bent just to imagine what childhood experience is actually like. And unfortunately, for both adults and children, no aspect of specialized training today is designed to spark the curiosity that could lead to such understanding.

While they are human like everyone else, child experts actually face a number of added challenges. The first is realizing that while their specialty training may have provided them with complex technical knowledge about theories and models of development, thinking, behavior, relating, pathology, and intervention techniques, *these abstractions are not actual children*. Moreover, specialized training and knowledge confer a sense of certainty and authority that often makes it quite difficult to see the obvious, especially when the obvious conflicts with cherished theories and practices.

So, if you agree that what we have written about in this book is essential to a realistic understanding of children, don't just allow this knowledge to coexist blissfully with the theories, models, and practices it challenges. Instead, *rethink your fundamentals* and ask yourself how much of what you've taken for granted may be wrong. We've had to do so, and it has made us much more observant and much more effective in everything we do clinically.

Do You Really Believe in Human Potential?

Americans tend to think that, of all the world's societies, we are the most committed to realizing human potential. After all, isn't American society enriched by all those immigrants who come to escape the constraints of other cultures? Isn't this country a place where anyone can rise to the top? And yet our view of the perfectibility of the individual may not be quite as positive as we like to think it is.

In 1991, curious about whether the American view of rampant childhood pathology was typical, we called Harold W. Stevenson, professor of psychology at the University of Michigan and one of this country's foremost experts on Asian education. Stevenson had just published the results of a ten-year prospective study of the academic achievement of matched groups of American, Japanese, and Chinese students. Since Stevenson and his team had personally interviewed and tested literally thousands of Asian students over the years and had visited countless classrooms in Japan, mainland China, and Taiwan, we asked him to tell us how much Attention Deficit Disorder, learning disabilities, and hyperactivity he had seen in Japanese classrooms. "Not only do you not see them," he replied, "but they have no vocabulary for them." Subsequently, we mentioned Stevenson's comments to a friend who was then director of a Midwest medical school child and adolescent psychiatry training program. "Aha!" he said. "Since they don't have the vocabulary to describe these disorders, they don't *see* them! So those kids never get identified." But that wasn't the case at all.

Actually, American educators and mental health professionals who visit Japanese preschools are shocked by the chaos and aggression that reign there, as well as by the fact that Japanese preschool teachers barely supervise and rarely intervene. Just as Stevenson had reassured me was the case, the Japanese have exactly the same range of spacey, drifting, spastic, inattentive, tuned-in, organized, disorganized, gentle, and aggressive children that we do. It's not that the Japanese have the good genes and we Americans have the bad genes; even within cultural styles, behavioral diversity is the norm. The important difference is that Japanese educators do not identify, diagnose, label, track, segregate, miseducate, and mistreat those chaotic preschoolers. Instead, *they change them,* beginning at age six.

As Merry White, a Boston University professor of anthropology who specializes in comparative studies of Japanese and American childhood, family, and education issues, puts it: "Americans believe in *fixed traits,* at the same time believing that you can at any time remake yourself; Japanese believe in *fluid possibilities,* at least within the range provided by one's ability to commit effort." The American notion of fixed traits results in the view that a disordered or disabled child will remain that way for the rest of his or her life. Thus, for example, the current boom in "Adult ADHD" and the increasing taste for widespread "mild" versions of serious or even dangerous psychiatric disorders.

In contrast to the Japanese, Americans accept perceived limitations. As Stevenson and his colleagues put it, one of the "most dismaying findings" in their ten-year prospective study was the fact that, while very few Chinese or Japanese mothers expressed satisfaction with their child's academic performance, 40 percent of American mothers were highly satisfied with their child's performance. Whereas American mothers accept their child's poor math performance on the grounds that the child is performing as well as his or her math ability will permit, Japanese mothers always see room for improvement—even when their child is receiving the highest marks. The result is that the *worst* Japanese schools boast higher math achievement than the *best* American schools.

Again, the lesson here is not that everything about Asian education in general, or Japanese education in particular, is better and should be embraced uncritically, but simply that *viewing human potential as inherently (i.e., genetically) limited results in tragically poor results*. This does NOT mean that we should "hurry" children and have them playing tennis and golf at age four. But it does mean that if an American child is "identified" as psychiatrically or educationally disordered or disabled, the expectations of educational and mental health professionals will be tailored to the concept of a lifelong disorder—not to the child's genuine potential.

We're paying a major price for our jaundiced view of the "genetically fixed" abilities of children—and not just in comparison to educational achievement in Japan. Data from the 1998 Third International Mathematics and Science Study show that we're lagging far behind the rest of the world in math achievement. Of the forty countries that participated in the eighth-grade portion of the study, *all but Cyprus and South Africa outperformed the United States in general math knowledge*—and this round didn't even include the Asian countries. Even eighth graders in those former Soviet bloc countries currently in the turmoil of massive change and economic and social instability outperformed their American counterparts.

The Importance of Language and Communication

Once you've decided that you really can make a difference in your work with children, think carefully about the role of language and communication in your field. Almost everything in education, mental health, and child-relevant research hinges vitally on communication, and much of that communication involves spoken language. This includes, but is hardly limited to:

- Interviewing children and parents
- Verbal classroom and clinic behavior and communication exchanges
- Understanding and complying with written instructions

- Oral instructions in the classroom or during educational or psychological testing
- Verbal behavior as judged by a routine mental status examination
- The informational aspects of teaching and the therapeutic aspects of clinical work

In fact, just about everything that child professionals do is mediated by language. Given the misunderstanding and miscommunication that characterize the everyday verbal exchanges between adults and children, how effective is communication in the professional setting and how often are the conclusions adults draw about children's cognitive-behavioral abilities accurate? An anecdote that could have come from tens of thousands of classrooms across the country highlights these important questions.

Just as we were finishing up this book, a mom brought in one of her eight-year-old's "failing" papers. The exercise, produced by the educational branch of a large American publisher, consisted of a picture to color and four sequential directions. The first three directions instructed the child to use three different and very specific colors to color very particular parts of three ships. The fourth direction was simply "Finish coloring the picture." This child followed the directions to the letter, using the proper colors in the proper order. But because he used some of the same colors to "finish coloring the picture"—the fourth direction—his paper came back marked with a huge F. "You see," the teacher told this child's mother, "your son has a central processing disorder. He can't process verbal sequences accurately." Yet nothing could have been further from the truth. Implicit in the instructions for this third-grade exercise was the assumption that all children would understand clearly that the rest of the drawing should be colored in with different colors—*even though that requirement was not specified.*

At first, it may seem preposterous to assert that many of the problems plaguing the childhood population today could be due to such mundane issues. But then a lot more preposterous things have been asserted before—such as that the earth is round and not flat. If you listen carefully to what you and your colleagues actually say to children, you'll discover that misunderstanding and miscommunication in the daycare center, the classroom, and the clinic are much more common than you might imagine. Repeated instances of this kind of adult-child miscommunication (in this case, the printed instructions) and misunderstanding (the teacher's interpretation) result over and over in basically normal, logical-minded children being saddled with damning psychoeducational diagnoses that lead nowhere. When a child like our third grader comes to be defined in terms of what he supposedly "cannot" understand and do, so do his educational or therapeutic opportunities. Understanding the logic of language and how children think can radically decrease the number of mislabeled, mistreated, and miseducated children who pour daily into our special education and mental health systems.

Cleaning Up Communication Styles

If you haven't already begun to pay special attention to what you say and how you say it, reread chapters 1, 2, and 3 and then put the principles we outlined there into action. Many teachers and clinicians have told us that they were amazed to see what different responses they got from their students or patients when they removed questions, empty statements, and other conventional "commands" from their verbal repertoire.

Before you decide that a student, subject, or patient has attentional or dissociative problems, listen carefully to yourself and examine your interactive style. So much of everyday language is dissociogenic and amnestogenic that it's a wonder kids follow any directions or remember much of anything! As you listen, you'll discover that the communication styles of both teachers (including childcare and preschool teachers) and child therapists—e.g., styles designed to "promote togetherness" or to "soften authoritarian tone" such as the Collective We and referring to oneself in the third person—often blur the boundaries of agency and responsibility. If you want understanding and compliance, be specific and be clear. Don't ask questions; instead, issue (polite) commands—and don't include yourself in the command. Don't forget that questions induce doubt and forgetting and are effectively suggestions NOT to remember, NOT to answer, NOT to comply. Repeated questions can be even more powerfully-if-subtly dissociogenic. So look for these styles in your own communication/interaction patterns. All the issues we addressed in chapters 6 through

8 apply just as much to daycare providers, teachers, clinicians, and researchers as they do to parents.

Challenge Apparently Pathological Behavior

There are two common ways of inadvertently promoting maladaptive behavior. The first and most common is to simply accept the behavior, i.e., to take appearances for granted. When child professionals accept surface appearances, they begin to accommodate to them. This involves adapting educational or clinical techniques and expectations to the child's condition—something that makes sense when the child is blind or wheelchair bound but not when the child appears not to understand, remember, do, etc. Such accommodations effectively define the child in *deficit* terms. Unfortunately, this practice has become the norm, as the title of a paper delivered at the 1987 annual meeting of the National Association for the Education of Young Children illustrates: "You Can't Help Me Until You Know What I Can't Do." However, as soon as you begin to think in such terms, you've effectively thrown in the towel. So, unless you think dissociation and attentional disorders are good for children, *don't accept, support, reinforce, or reify them!* Instead, challenge them.

Challenging problem behaviors does not mean being confrontational or telling someone that their symptoms aren't real. It means *testing them out.* This can be done as simply as by changing one's communication style from an empty statement/questioning approach that allows for repeated logical responses without conscious awareness to a polite command style in which "Tell me . . ." replaces "Can you tell me . . . ?" or "Do you remember . . . ?"

And use simple common sense. If a child looks like she's having a petit mal seizure, simply blow in her eyes. If she blinks, she has an intact corneal reflex. If she has an intact corneal reflex, she's not seizing. It's that simple. The world of educational and psychological ability and functioning is no different: every time you get a child to tell you something that he supposedly doesn't know or to do something he supposedly can't do, every time you succeed in getting a child to remember material for which he is supposedly amnestic, you have successfully challenged symptomatic behavior. Gently challenging appearances is very effective and costs nothing.

The second most common way of inadvertently promoting maladaptive behavior is by allowing it to persist for the purpose of "documenting" the behavior. If you want to reinforce maladaptive behavior, use behavior rating scales and quasi-diagnostic instruments like the Child Dissociative Checklist (CDC). Many of the categorical items on the CDC represent variants of normative childhood behaviors, all of which can be influenced by intervening adults. The rest represents target behaviors to be challenged or behavioral clues to indicate potentially solvable problems, not "developmental psychopathology" to be documented—often for extended periods. Many of the behaviors on the CDC will respond quickly to signs that an adult cares enough to pay attention, follow up the leads, and intervene.

Don't Forget Why You Work with Children

Always keep in mind *why* you're working with children. Whether you work in an educational or clinical setting, if you want to validate pathology, then use rating scales, checklists, and diagnostic instruments. If, on the other hand, you actually want to *change* problem behavior, then treat children as children, keep your expectations high, challenge symptomatic behavior, and pay attention to the nature of childhood experience—just as parents can do on a daily basis.

Make Use of Structure,
Rules, and Boundaries

Over the last fifteen years, we've visited many training facilities and talked with many teachers and clinicians. One of the things we've noticed in settings ranging from university psychiatry departments to private offices is the lack of structure that is meaningful for children. Having a corner in your office or a playtherapy room full of all the recommended paraphernalia—from sand trays to dolls, clay, and toy guns—may represent meaningful structure to the adult, but, for children, it's just a bunch of stuff. If you're going to be as much in charge of your own space as we feel that parents should be of theirs, then don't assume that children possess some miraculous inborn knowledge of what to do what all that stuff. Adults who count on some sort of generic, mystical "healing power of play" are counting on little children to provide the structure and content of a process of which the adult should be in control.

Everything in your space—whether your classroom or your office/ therapy room—is part of your structure. How you use the contents of your space represents your rules and boundaries. If you want to capitalize on the adaptive self-organizational potential of children, you need to be in charge of that space. Often, when we do workshops for our clinical colleagues, someone will protest that all the rules governing the "therapeutic space" that we outlined in *Healing the Hurt Child* are unrealistic "in the real world." Two of the thirteen rules, in particular, tend to elicit protests:

- Everything in the playtherapy room has a place and that place never changes.
- Everything in the playtherapy room should be put back in its place at the end of the session. Although the child is not required to do this personally, he or she should remain in the room until the original order is restored.

While our colleagues understand the rationale for not letting a child leave a disordered space, they think our first rule above is totally unrealistic. "You just don't understand what it's like when you have eight or nine therapists using the same therapy room," we've been told. "We can't decide *what* to keep in the playroom, let alone *where* to keep it." Well, we can understand what it's like because both of us have worked in settings where a single playtherapy room was used by many staff members. But there is a solution, one that's based on the *child's experience of the space*, not on adults'.

Since you share your therapy setting with many other staff members, you can't control the hour-to-hour, day-to-day order of the playtherapy room, so don't worry about it—it's simply beyond your control. What you *can* control, however, is the experience of each of your individual little patients. Let's say that you work with fifteen children each week. Since we know (from chapters 6 and 8) that children are normative dissociators and that they can easily tune out whatever doesn't interest them, simply pick out four items that play a meaningful role in their therapies—*and then make sure that those four items are in the same place at the beginning of each child's therapy hour.* You will find that the kids you work with will tune out the ambient chaos and tune in to the meaningful consistency, continuity, and predictability that you have created. Just as there is always some aspect of human potential that can be mobilized, there is always some range of freedom in your control over the environment. Don't give up because the overall picture is chaotic. Instead, pick out those points of potential stability and continuity of experience—and then exploit them.

Also, don't assume that you can't have a significant impact just because a child's environment is chaotic. Children are like sponges: they manage to soak up whatever crumbs of creative experience and stability may be available. We have found it possible to work with children from unbelievably chaotic and unpredictable environments. Most of these children tune in to our consistent and predictable structure and pick up right where they left off the week before. If you're able to gain the understanding of a caring parent or other responsible adult, then aspects of predictable structure can be introduced into the child's home experience, and the two work synergistically. But, even if you go it alone as a daycare worker, teacher, or therapist, assume that many of the children you work with will profit from your structure and your consistency simply because that experience is now part of their knowledge base. They will build upon it on their own, and that experience will make it easier for them to recognize and utilize similar experiences in the world.

How to Assess the "Latest" Findings

Despite their specialized training, professionals who work with children face the same challenge as parents when it comes to assessing the barrage of new theories, research data, and "latest" techniques. Just to assess the accuracy of the latest science news, even those who have access to excellent university libraries (or the Internet) would have to spend an immense amount of time verifying, double-checking, and searching out competing or contradictory findings, so what should child professionals do? Simple: think critically about any "authoritative" and "accurate" research data or any expert opinion or advice—and be sure that the foundation for doing so is the same realistic and commonsense understanding of children that we think is so important for parents.

For example, in the midst of a rash of school shootings, media reports about some of the youngest children alleged to have committed murder indicated that experts were saying that seven-year-olds were not developmentally capable of understanding the permanency of death and, consequently, should not be judged by adult standards. That statement sounds quite reasonable because it is consistent with the view that has been held since Freud's famous statement in *The Interpretation of Dreams* that anyone who takes seriously that children can wish the actual death of another "has failed to bear in mind that a child's idea of being 'dead' has nothing much in common with ours apart from the word." It is, after all, what the experts say. But how does that assertion look if we put it back into a realistic context and try to imagine how a child would act upon such a belief? If a seven-year-old really believed that death wasn't permanent, then he or she should expect the dead person to return to life, to get up and walk, to poop and pee and do any of those things that living people can do. Is that what seven-year-olds *really* believe? It is, after all, what you find in the books, and it may even be what some young children say in response to a question. But would their behavior be consistent with such a belief in the impermanence of death? THAT's the answer to the question.

Now, why wasn't there a cry of protest from the community of child experts when one of their own was shown repeatedly on national television maintaining a view that really makes no sense? *Because real children are not the point of reference for expert knowledge about children's development, thinking, behavior, capabilities, etc.* So if you want to think critically about the latest findings, theories, explanations, or recommendations that flood the media and the professional world alike, make a realistic understanding of children your point of reference.

Last But Most Important—
Don't Get Wiped Out

One significant difference between the experience of parents and education and mental health professionals—especially the "front line" professionals such as daycare workers, teachers, and mental health center workers—is that parents see only a few children while you see the same thing over and over and over. In fact, the seemingly endless stream of uninterested, disorganized children, often from disadvantaged, chaotic, or violent homes, can be immensely demoralizing.

We see the same children and families that you do—but what keeps our heads above water is the fact that we get to see the vast majority of children we work with get significantly better. If we didn't, we would find something else to do. We hope that the perspective that we have tried to present in this book, and the very real and often simple things that you can do to make things better, will help you keep your head above water, too.

Appendix

Parents Ask About the Five Minutes

We have consistently found over the years that whether or not parents do the Five Minutes determines how quickly and how effectively our clinical work proceeds. We even tell parents that our goal is to put ourselves out of business, to make ourselves useless—so *speed up the process, do the Five Minutes!*

When we find ourselves bogged down even though we're dealing with bright, caring parents and adaptively responsive kids, first we ask ourselves if there's anything we've missed—then we ask whether they're still doing the Five Minutes. Most of the time, they aren't. Once the parents resume the Five Minutes and stick with it, our therapy picks up again.

Parents Ask Questions

Of all the complex issues we've raised with parents over the years, the Five Minutes has generated by far the most questions. Some of the questions parents have asked are about the structure and purpose of the Five Minutes, but most are about how to deal with situations unique to each child and family. The actual structure of the Five Minutes is really very simple. Yet each question reminds us that even simple things are experienced within complex human situations in which apparently "minor" changes can result in major challenges for those involved. Each question also provides an opportunity to imagine a challenge without having to actually experience it, which makes it easy to deal with similar circumstances, should they arise.

At first, we were frustrated by the repetitiousness in some of these questions. "Some people just don't seem to get it," we said to each other. But then we thought back to our own clinical experience and realized that all one has to do to make the old completely new is simply to change the context. And, in life, context is always in flux. This means that we all have to learn what appears to be the same lesson many times in many different contexts. So be patient with what may appear to be the same question asked again in just a slightly different way. For the parents who asked these questions, each subtle difference was experienced as a brand-new challenge to understanding or problem-solving. And be patient as well with questions whose answers seem to be glaringly obvious—some of these questions were asked by parents with M.D.'s or Ph.D.'s.

When is the best time to start the Five Minutes? The same as for starting a diet or a savings account—today.

Is there a time of day that is best or worst? There are no "best" times, but there are certainly "worst" times. These tend to be when everyone is feeling a lot of pressure—typically mornings when everyone is rushing to get ready for school and work. Many parents like to do the Five Minutes in the evening, partially because bedtime isn't a deadline like the beginning of work or school. If you do choose this time, don't leave the Five Minutes to the very last moment because then it becomes confused with bedtime rituals. And don't worry that it has to be done at exactly the same time every day—just make it regular and reliable.

We already have family meetings and we even talk as a family every evening at sit-down dinner. Do we still need the Five Minutes? Yes. First, don't change a thing as far as family meetings and your sit-down family dinner are concerned. They're a marvelous part of family life that has all but disappeared from the American scene. But they don't serve the same *individual* needs as the Five Minutes. Children need a unique, private relationship with each parent as much as a communal relationship with the family.

You've just formalized what I already do with my child, so why formalize it? Two reasons: First, given that you're seeking answers in this book, because what you're doing informally probably isn't working. Second, as we know from religious tradition, *ritual makes any experience greater than the sum of its parts*. So does the Five Minutes. Besides, its simple structure, rules, and boundaries make it much more powerful over time than haphazard daily experiences.

What if we've already talked for hours that day and the conversation was rich and meaningful? Think of the Five Minutes as a "communication and understanding generator." It starts the process and keeps it going. While some children may confide meaningfully only during the Five Minutes, many will begin to open up outside that highly boundaried brief period of time. So don't turn off the "generator."

Do I need to do the Five Minutes with all my children? Absolutely. The Five Minutes is not a specialized "therapy technique." It's a relationship builder and an easy, efficient way to promote effective communication. These are nonspecifics that every child needs and deserves.

Isn't three a bit too young to start doing the Five Minutes? A dad thought our Five Minutes was a great idea for his five-year-old son but then said, "Jack's got a three-year-old sister. She's too young for this to make any sense, isn't she?"

If you want your child to literally grow into life taking for granted that she can always talk to you and that she is always free to tell you anything, start the Five Minutes early. For many children, three is just fine. Your three-year-old won't talk to you in the same way that your five-year-old will, but, by age five, the Five Minutes will have become an integral and natural part of your now-five-year-old's life. Initially, knowing that you are there, that she has your full and undivided attention, is actually more important to your child than anything she might tell you. Remember, many children don't communicate openly with their parents because they don't want to embarrass them or hurt their feelings. Nothing conveys your openness, your willingness to hear whatever your child has to say, and your comfort with whatever may be said more than our little daily ritual. Trusting that it's safe to be honest and open with you will become part and parcel of your child's relationship with you.

Should both parents do the Five Minutes? Absolutely. Remember, the purpose of the Five Minutes is to promote communication and build a relationship between the child and parent, so that means *each* parent should do his or her Five Minutes *alone* with each child.

I know you're supposed to do the Five Minutes individually with each child, but I have a special case. Can I do the Five Minutes with my twins together? No. In fact, you should treat each of your children as a unique individual, whether they're twins or singletons. If you promote or encourage sameness in your twins, they will be much more vulnerable to the negative experiences that life deals each of us individually. The older years, especially, can be horrendously painful for twins whose identities are linked. When one becomes ill or handicapped, both suffer. When one dies, the other may fall apart.

In fact, if you know that you're carrying twins, think about these issues *well before* your twins are born. It is more difficult to get identical twins, who are reared together and see each other all the time, to develop separate, individual, and autonomous identities if you dress them identically from birth on. So start prepared. Read *The Nature and Nurture of Twins* and *Twins in the Family* by Dr. Elizabeth Bryan.

What if I'm divorced and the kids spend half the week with their father and half with me? Many parents and children would find that kind of teeter-totter lifestyle hard to live with, but some accommodate to it quite well. The continuity can be maintained simply by doing the Five Minutes daily by phone.

I only see my child every other weekend, so what's the use of the Five Minutes? Two weeks is a long time for teenagers and older children and a *very* long time for young children. Even young children know that, under normal circumstances, parents and children see one another and talk to one another every day. If you live in the same community and don't maintain regular *daily* contact, younger children especially will feel that they simply aren't important and that you literally forget them during the time between visits.

So, when you can't do the Five Minutes in person, do it by phone—and, of course, daily if you can. Coordinate with your child's other parent or guardian so that both sides understand the purpose of the calls and so that privacy can be assured, then explain the process to your child. It can only enrich the relationship.

My daughter tells me things about what her father (or mother) does that I never knew about. What should I do? If you feel that your child, and not your ex-spouse, is trying to make you feel bad and guilty, then simply tell her that you understand how angry and upset at you she must be. (And, remember, this is not an admission of guilt, only an expression of your understanding.) This is all the more important if the other spouse is NOT taking any responsibility. If your ex-spouse denies all responsibility and blames everything on you, and you don't validate your child's feelings, things will only get worse because she will pressure you to fill that responsibility vacuum.

Finally, parents occasionally do learn of dangerous or illegal activities during the Five Minutes. In that case, do what's appropriate with regard to custody, visitation, or even law enforcement issues.

Should a stepparent or permanent live-in do the Five Minutes? Yes—but with a very important caveat. Relationships should be real and enduring. *No one who is not going to be a permanent part of the child's life should do the Five Minutes.* So, if you know that the relationship with your spouse or live-in is shaky, and that he or she is probably on the way out, do NOT promote an *artificial relationship* that will only create problems for you and your child when that "relationship" collapses.

My child can't wait for the Five Minutes. He talks the entire time, but he never says anything of substance. Do I just sit there and listen to him have fun saying nothing forever? Many parents, while saying that they would give anything for their child to talk to them, are really quite defensive. Because they're uncomfortable with, or even afraid of, what their child might say to them, they tend to fill up the time with questions or commentary. The result is that nothing of significance ever gets said. To minimize the possibility that this will happen routinely, we purposefully designed the Five Minutes to be unfair—"fairness" meaning an equal part for each—and unbalanced. It really is *the child's time* to say whatever is on his mind, not the adult's. Most of the time, the structure of the Five Minutes works quite well and children start to open up to their parents.

If, however, you're comfortable hearing whatever your child has to say, and your child's just not talking, it's okay to stimulate discussion. Unless you know of something significant that your child has avoided talking about, start with the day. Get him to talk about school, but with prompting, not specific questions. *Tell me the best thing that happened in school today. Tell me the most interesting thing that happened in school today. Tell me the WORST thing that happened in school today.* Or make it more general: *Tell me the best thing that happened to you today*, etc.

There are always things in every child's life that remain unacknowledged and never get shared. You can use the Five Minutes to revisit those experiences that your child has never shared with you. Just say something like "Tell me how you felt when . . ." or "You must have really been sad when . . ." or "You must have been really upset when . . ." Even if your child replies, "I didn't feel anything" (which you know is a bunch of baloney), your question communicates, more than any verbal reassurance could, that you're tuned-in and that you care.

Remember too that by issuing a command instead of asking a question, you greatly increase the likelihood that your child will think about the issue you just raised or the event you just described. That's already a major step in the right direction. It also makes it harder for your child to dissociate emotional responses—and to tune you out. Your purpose is not to define your child's feelings or to tell him what he thinks, but to let him know that you really do understand him, that you know he has strong feelings about significant events in his life, and that you really do want to hear about them. If you keep your "questions" open-ended ("Tell me how you felt . . . ," "You must have been upset . . . ," "It must have really affected you . . ."), you won't have to worry about being overly suggestive—or even about being completely wrong. What will register on your child is that you care, that you know he has feelings, and that you respect those feelings. If you were wrong, he'll probably tell you. Maybe not during the Five Minutes, but eventually.

However, don't start filling up the time with such questions. Give your child time to learn that your presence and your attention are reliable.

What if my child just sits there? Whether your child talks or not, your comfortable continuing presence communicates your openness, your willingness to listen, and your commitment to your child. When the Five Minutes is up, just say something like "Well, our Five Minutes is up. I bet you'll have *lots* to share with me next time!" Don't get discouraged. Keep your tone of voice positive and encouraging. That's all you need. In our experience, nearly every child will begin to open up if the parent doesn't give up prematurely.

When it's time to do the Five Minutes, my son just goes in his bedroom, slams the door, and won't even let me in. What should I do? First of all, don't take it personally and don't get upset. Such behavior is (1) a dramatic attempt to push your buttons and (2) a sign that sharing real feelings is difficult. So just pull up a chair and say, "I'm right here, outside the door. We're still having our Five Minutes." If your child looks out the door to see if you're still there, say something like "I see you're thinking of joining me"—even if he has one of those "God, are you still here!" looks on his face. Just sit there until the time has passed. Then say something like "Time's up. The Five Minutes is over. I'm sure looking forward to being able to do it on the same side of the door next time!"

Notice that we didn't suggest that you say "I'm sure looking forward to being able to do it *together* next time" because that would mean that you had allowed your child to define you as "apart" by going in his room and slamming the door. Instead, you're actively defining your relationship as "being together"—even when there's a wall between you. This may sound picky, but every time you give in to these negative reactions, you add another negative brick to the structure of a negative relationship. On the other hand, every time you define the relationship glass as "half full," you are supporting a process that will eventually bring you closer in a literal sense.

If your child reacts to the Five Minutes by slamming the door to his bedroom, chances are that he's slamming other literal and figurative doors on you the rest of the time. Remember that the Five Minutes is not a cure-all. It's part of an overall relationship—and an overall strategy. We assume that you are paying close attention to all the other issues we've raised in the book and making many changes in your communication and relationship style as well. Remember too that with such angry-reactive children, shifting the emphasis from frustration and anger to sadness and the sharing of feelings is very important.

STOP! We know what's going through your mind: "Won't this sound *awfully phony* to a child, especially an older child or an adolescent? In fact," you may be thinking, "this is right out of a sitcom!"

> The dad announces that he and the kid are going to have a new kind of "quality time." The kid blows him off with a "Been listening to Dr. Laura again, huh?" and the audience chuckles. The kid goes in his room and closes the door, so Dad sits down on the floor and leans up against the wall outside the door and says, "I'm right out here. We're still having our Five Minutes."
>
> At this point, Mom comes by and says, "What happened to you? Didn't make it to the bathroom?" More canned laughter.
>
> "No," says the dad, "it's a new communication technique I'm trying out."
>
> "With what, *the wall?*" More laughter and the scene dissolves . . .

Starting the Five Minutes with a resistant, off-putting kid may resemble a sitcom, but the outcome doesn't have to. On the sitcom, the scene moves on and that's that. The dad gets dissed, wises up quickly, and drops the whole thing before he has the chance to feel more embarrassed. But what happens if you play the scene out that way in real life? Your teenager does a totally self-defeating Double Whammy. He both wins and loses in the blink of an eye. First, he goes instantly for the embarrassment jugular and squeezes until you cry uncle. Then he quickly puts your sincerity and commitment to the test—and you fold, feeling like a self-conscious idiot, before you even get started.

This is, deep down inside, just what they don't want you to do.

So *don't give up! Just survive the brilliant attempt to make you feel like a clumsy idiot.*

Treat such moments as a fascinating—if momentarily uncomfortable— challenge to your creativity, not as a categorical rejection. Say something like "Hey, it may seem silly to you, but I'm serious. I want to know what's on your mind." In our experience, parents who didn't cave in under such challenges have had much more success in establishing a meaningful and productive daily encounter with even the most off-putting of kids.

What if my child NEVER talks during the Five Minutes? It depends, so let's divide the nontalkers into two groups.

First, the genuine nontalkers. In our experience with hundreds of children whose parents have done the Five Minutes over the years, only two or three *never* talked at all. But even these children began to open up outside of the Five Minutes. If you treat the Five Minutes as a motor that drives a process of communication and relationship-building, and not as an end in and of itself, then it doesn't really matter whether the child talks during that brief five-minute period of togetherness.

Second, the talkers who just aren't talking. These are children who will talk to you if you find the key. We don't introduce this concept or suggest ways to deal with this kind of silence until we've become convinced that the parent understands the process of the Five Minutes and isn't trying to fill up the silence. *Only then* do we suggest that the parent become more active by bringing up issues that the parent suspects or knows were significant in the child's experience. "You must have been really disappointed when . . ." the parent can say, or "I'll bet it really hurt your feelings when . . ." These comments—notice again that they're NOT questions—let the child know that the parent is tuned-in and has already understood that whatever has happened had an impact on the child. They are also implicit suggestions that the child should think about those issues and share his or her feelings. This makes it much more likely that the child will think about them, whether or not the child actually shares them aloud with the parent. Many parents find that this is all it takes to get their child to begin to talk. Once it does, it's important not to fall into the habit of prompting all the time.

The Five Minutes makes perfect sense to me, but, for some reason, I just haven't been able to get it started. I don't know why, but I actually find myself avoiding even the thought of doing the Five Minutes. Hectic lives aside, the most common reason why parents find it hard to start the Five Minutes is apprehension. Many more parents than you might imagine are actually afraid to find out what their child really thinks—of them, of the world, and of themselves. Many parents are afraid that their child will reproach them for things they have done or have failed to do. Others don't want to tell their children that they feel they are powerless to make things better. Some parents feel guilty about the amount of time they've given their children or about their lack of emotional availability because they're wrapped up in a new job, a new relationship, illness, or even depression. Some parents fear that their children really don't like them. Others, mothers especially, just don't want their children to feel emotional pain, so they avoid it altogether. They may fear that beginning the Five Minutes will open a Pandora's box of losses, fears, and unhealed wounds that they cannot change.

Acknowledging your child's feelings is NOT the same as taking responsibility for them or agreeing to make reparations. None of that is necessary. Fortunately, parents don't have to fix the world in order to make things much, much better. What children need most—what everyone needs most—is simply to be acknowledged, understood, and cared for.

My son really *hates* the Five Minutes. Why should I persist in doing something that he absolutely detests? What child likes immunizations? How many kids are beating down the school doors trying to get in at the end of August? *Don't stop being a benevolent authority in your child's life just because he doesn't like, or even hates, something.* So, once again, treat this as an initial challenge to see whether you're committed to both him and real communication. Lots of kids *say* they "really hate" the Five Minutes at the very beginning, but, if parents don't give up, very few continue with their protests.

My child no longer has lots of earthshaking things to talk about, but he can talk your ears off! The Five Minutes is just what its name implies: a *five-minute* period each day that your child can count on. However, it loses its special privileged character if it becomes nothing more than a time to chat. If you enjoy spending a good hour every day talking with your child, that's fine—but don't get into a habit of listening to empty talk whose only purpose is to keep you there. That's not productive. So if your child's just chatting because he or she just loves talking to you, it's perfectly fine to say, "Okay, our Five Minutes is over" and bring it to an end. Do so with gentle firmness, and don't feel guilty.

My nine-year-old has suddenly stopped talking to me. What happened?
You've probably stopped doing the Five Minutes. Even though we're very careful to point out that the Five Minutes is, first and foremost, *a relationship* and *an experience of predictability, reliability, and openness*, many parents still treat it as a gimmick. Gimmicks are supposed to work like keys: Use it once, open the door, and you don't need it again. Relationships last over time. So does the Five Minutes.

We've had many parents call up several months after completing therapy and say that they needed to come back because their child's behavior had "regressed." They, too, have stopped the Five Minutes. When we ask why, they reply, "Because we thought it was part of the therapy." "No," we stress, "*it's part of the relationship*. Start up the Five Minutes again and give us a call in two or three weeks to let us know how things are going." After restarting the Five Minutes, most of the time these families do not need to return.

Each of my two sons wants to be first to do the Five Minutes every night, so we always end up in a struggle. First of all, don't leave the Five Minutes until the last thing every night. Look for ways in which your sons' schedules vary, and then see if you can find separate times when competition isn't possible.

If separate times during the day aren't practical, simply have your boys take turns being first. You can alternate days or weeks. We suggest weeks because it's too easy to lose track of alternating days. It's also easier for children to be patient if a (relatively short) block of time has a particular structure.

We also suggest that you make taking turns a family policy. This will also help avoid the "I got here first!" battle over who gets to sit in the front seat of the car (assuming, of course, that your children are old and tall enough to meet your state's legal requirements for sitting there).

What if my child really wants physical contact? Should I withhold it?
Listen to your words: you've turned yourself into a "withholding parent"
instead of simply being a benevolent authority. This is a variation on the
"What if my child *hates* the Five Minutes." Just tell your child that there's
plenty of time during the rest of the day for hugging or sitting in your lap.
Don't let yourself feel like the Grinch Who Stole Christmas just because
you structure your child's experience and don't give in to his or her
"wants."

I feel like I'm being asked for a confession during the Five Minutes.
Yes, it can certainly feel that way. But when you say, "I understand how
you feel," you are validating your child's feelings, not agreeing that their
assertions or even their recollections are correct and accurate. When you
say something that sounds even more specific, such as, "I certainly do
understand how upset you are," you're still not taking responsibility for
what the child is upset about. You're only conveying that you really do
understand their feelings. Even if they're 100 percent wrong about the literal facts of the matter—and you don't provoke a standoff by pointing
this out—you will have actually increased the likelihood that, sometime
later, they'll come to you and say, "I know it didn't really happen that
way. I was just really upset."

**My kid isn't just critical, he knows I've got to sit there, keep my mouth
shut, and just listen to his disrespect during the Five Minutes.** Not at
all. While it's true that the Five Minutes is your child's time to say what's
on his mind, not the adult's, and while it's true that he can say "anything," *he should say it respectfully*. Remind your child that, while you're
there to hear whatever he has to say, he needs to express himself in a
respectful manner. Here we have structure, rules, and boundaries again.
One of the rules is that he needs to be respectful, just as you need to listen without explaining, excusing, or telling him that he's wrong to think
what he thinks or feel what he feels. Take a moment to discuss this with
your child outside the Five Minutes. Don't fill up the Five Minutes with
discussions of protocol.

Okay, so I don't explain, excuse, or clarify. What DO I do? The Five
Minutes is not about *doing*. It's about being there, listening, and under-

standing, so there's no need for you to *do* anything. In fact, if you get that uncomfortable with what seems to be "doing nothing," then imagine how antsy your child is bound to be! Even our piddly little Five Minutes works to calm jumpy, spastic cognitive-behavioral styles.

My child brings up real-world, practical problems about home, school, etc. Shouldn't I offer solutions? Don't confuse *solving a real-world problem* with the purpose of the Five Minutes—to create an environment in which your child feels understood and accepted. However, one of the real benefits of the Five Minutes is that parents eventually begin to hear about genuinely important issues that, otherwise, they might never have learned about.

A young child who had previously only complained that his teacher was "mean" told his mother during the Five Minutes that his teacher would routinely make a spectacle of crumpling up a child's paper that she found unacceptable and throwing it in the wastebasket beside her desk. *During the Five Minutes*, the mom let her seven-year-old know that she understood how crushed he must feel when that happens to him. *Outside of the Five Minutes*, the mom, armed with the information she had gained there, called other mothers and discovered that her son was not alone in being extremely disturbed by the teacher's behavior. She pursued the matter with the principal, and her son was moved to another class, where he flourished. The teacher in question was not rehired the following year.

My son does anything he can to bug me during the Five Minutes— comes over to where I'm seated and stares at me, picks up a toy and starts to play, or starts drawing and just ignores me. If this kind of behavior is occurring during the Five Minutes, it is bound to be occurring during the rest of the day. This means that structure, rules, and boundaries have probably gone by the wayside during the day and/or that your child is really angry at you for something. So, first of all, rethink the rest of the day. Put your structure, rules, and boundaries back into place. Then—during the same day, of course—gently remind your child what the rules are for the Five Minutes. Do NOT get into any kind of struggle. Just stick it out until the Five Minutes is up and remind your child that you expect that he'll find it easier to tell you what's *really* on his mind tomorrow.

If this disrespectful Space Invader behavior occurs *only* during the Five Minutes, simply take advantage of an appropriate time during the day to bring up an issue that you feel may have been a source of hurt, anger, disappointment, or frustration for your child. Don't link the subject to the Five Minutes, and don't go searching for possible upsetting events. Often, you will be able to determine what is bothering your child. In any case, just continue on as usual during the Five Minutes.

I started doing the Five Minutes three months ago. All of a sudden, I realized that my daughter isn't bugging me all the time anymore. Is there a connection? Many parents complain that their children do things "for attention" but fail to grasp the significance of their own observation. Once children begin to take the Five Minutes for granted, they have begun to learn that *they can count on their parent's attention every single day*. Once that certainty starts to become established, "attention-seeking" behavior often decreases dramatically. So give your child the attention he or she needs—in the most efficient, time-sparing manner possible: do the Five Minutes.

What if my teenager tells me about something—like stealing at school or shoplifting—that would normally result in parental action? Such disclosures can have two very different meanings. If your child or teenager discloses during the Five Minutes that they've shoplifted or stolen *and* also tells you that they don't know why *and* that they feel bad about it, then the Five Minutes has done what it's supposed to do: make it possible for your child to trust you and share with you.

When children steal things that they could have had for the asking, it's safe to conclude that they feel unworthy or don't believe that you would respond positively. Even when children think that they are being shortchanged materially in comparison to their peers, there can still be a significant component of not getting what they need from parents in terms of the relationship. This now opens up a whole new area for discussion. To make sure that you're not sending double messages, help your child or teenager to figure out how to return the stolen property or to compensate for the loss if it has been disposed of or used up. We have found that, under such circumstances, most of the time those from whom the child or adolescent stole are understanding and forgiving.

On the other hand, if your older child or teenager knows that trouble is about to erupt as a result of stealing or shoplifting and is quite purpose-fully using the Five Minutes in a manipulative fashion, then simply make it perfectly clear that you are calling a halt to the Five Minutes because this is NOT a Five Minutes issue. Say something like "Time out! We'll do our Five Minutes later. Right now, we're going to deal with what you've just told me." And remember, *understanding and acceptance do NOT get a person off the hook of personal and legal responsibility.*

Occasionally parents are deceived at times like this. However, we have found that most of the time parents have little difficulty telling the difference between a psychologically meaningful revelation and manipu-lation. (If this sounds too facile, remember that the Five Minutes is not a cure-all—*it's part of your relationship with your child.* At times like this, just be thankful that you found out what's going on. But don't expect the Five Minutes to solve these complex problems.)

What do I do if my child tells me about something hurtful a friend did to him and about the revenge he has planned? If your child is a pre-teen who doesn't already have a history of violence and habitual rule-breaking, then just let your child know that you understand how hurt or disappointed he or she may be. If, on the other hand, you're deal-ing with a kid who doesn't care and who *will* hurt someone else, under-stand his or her feelings—and then deal with it practically (which may involve notifying authorities or other parents to be on the lookout for trouble).

What if my teenager tells me about potentially dangerous choices such as drug use, riding with friends who drive drunk, unsafe sex (for some parents, any sex), being mistreated by a boyfriend, etc.? Then, once again, the Five Minutes has been effective—you've learned something extremely important about what's happening in your teenager's life. Now you can help him or her address those issues, each of which will probably lead to other important things the two of you can work out together.

My daughter called at 10:00 P.M. to do her Five Minutes while spend-ing the night with a friend. I'm concerned that she's become too dependent upon this five-minute thing. Our first question is: Why didn't you do the Five Minutes *before* you drove your daughter over to her friend's house to spend the night? It sounds like you've dropped the relationship-communication ball. Second, your reference to the Five Minutes as "this five-minute thing" suggests that you don't feel comfortable with it—which may be related to why you aren't consistent about doing it.

Finally, you give us a very big clue as to what this is really all about in your concern that your daughter may be becoming "too dependent." Your daughter isn't dependent upon the Five Minutes—*she's dependent upon you.* That, we suspect, is probably what is making you uncomfortable.

We would suggest that you give the whole subject of dependency some thought. Is dependency good or bad? Can any of us grow up and become successfully autonomous and independent without first experiencing healthy and reliable dependency?

"Dependent" means *hanging from* or, more colloquially, *hanging on to*—pendants are things that hang from a chain. Babies hang on to mothers, vines hang on to trellises, and both become strong *as a result of*—not in spite of—that creative dependency.

Ask yourself if your experience of childhood dependency was not a safe, secure, and creative one. Do you still secretly wish that you could be completely dependent on someone, that someone would accept and care for you unconditionally? Or do you believe that dependency is a trap—that, if you give in to it, you'll never get free?

The most positive and productive way to look at your situation is simply to say that your daughter clearly cares about you and misses her daily time with you. Capitalize on that care. Use the Five Minutes to build a strong relationship of openness and trust. If you do—and if we're right about any of the above—you'll discover that *your sense of wholeness and autonomy* grows as you do for your daughter what was never done for you.

Since we started this, my child wants her Five Minutes every time she's upset. Sharp kid! Your child is clearly a short-term strategic thinker. This reaction is actually very common in bright children who have discovered that their parents will really listen to them and who want to take advantage of the fact. All you have to do is to say, "No, we'll do our Five Minutes later like we always do, so just save what you want to say until then." Be neutral and matter-of-fact. Your child will discover through the process that the Five Minutes is not a way to have a captive audience and to drive her point home, but rather an ongoing relationship in which she can trust that you will always listen and understand.

I know this is a technique for kids, but can I do the Five Minutes with my spouse or partner? Absolutely. Many parents we've worked with over the years have used the Five Minutes with each other. There are differences, however, and some modifications are necessary.

First, the main difference: spouses and partners find it even harder *just to listen and not explain or defend* with each other than they do with children. Perhaps this is because spouses and partners find it easier to see the positive parenting or therapeutic value in listening and validating when it comes to children. Parents look to children, not so much for validation, but for signs that they're doing the right thing. Spouses and partners are more like children than parents, each looking to the other for fundamental validation. Doing the Five Minutes according to the rules actually requires some instant maturity on the part of spouses and partners. Working those rules out can be a good experience.

The biggest change has to do with the daily nature of the Five Minutes. It's almost impossible for each adult to have his or her Five Minutes on the same day because it's very hard for the second spouse not to use it as a rebuttal to the previous Five Minutes. Any spouse saintly enough not to say out loud what he or she was forced to think silently probably doesn't have a communication problem in the first place. We've found that such "You had your turn, but now it's my turn" versions of the Five Minutes make things worse, not better. The solution is simply to alternate days. After a period of doing a formal Five Minutes, adults who really get something out of the process become better listeners and more able to provide the support and validation that is often all that is needed. When this happens, communication styles change and the Five Minutes per se may no longer be needed. This change in how you deal with communication is for adults, however, NOT for children. Parent-child relationships are very different, so don't ever stop the Five Minutes with your child.

Endnotes

Denis M. Donovan, M.D., M.Ed.

1. "What Did I Just Say!?!"

Page 1:   " *'Do you want a spanking?'* " We're often told that the experts are saying that no one spanks anymore or that the trend is definitely away
from spanking and corporal punishment and toward informed behavioral
management techniques. The experts must not be walking the aisles at Wal-
Mart or Toys " Я " Us.

3. Childhood Thinking and the Logic of Language

Page 22:   "*. . . children are, in fact, logical thinkers . . .*" We introduced the distinction
between the logic of language and childhood thinking, on the one hand, and
Piaget's notion of "formal operations" in chapters 1 and 2 of *Healing the Hurt
Child* (Donovan and McIntyre 1990). Conventional meaning equates logic
and *reasonableness of thought*, whereas logic is actually a process of inference
and demonstration that operates upon a relatively closed system of interre-
lated propositions that may or may not be true. To this day, educational
and mental health professionals continue to confuse *logical reasoning* and
reasonable thinking, a confusion that has a very long tradition—but
one that has certainly become part and parcel of what it means to think
"correctly."

26:    "*Marilyn, Saddam Hussein, and the Pasta Roni box . . .*" Words can mean
whatever we want them to mean, thanks to what Ferdinand de Saussure, the
founder of modern linguistics, termed the *arbitrariness of the linguistic sign*
(Saussure 1972/1916). Because word meanings are arbitrary, they change

over time and across contexts. This is another reason why the dogged emphasis of American educational and mental health professionals on "correct" language makes little sense. For an example of the experts failing to understand the communicative and interpersonal styles of children, see Cantwell and Baker (1987). Cantwell and Baker confuse language and speech, correct grammar and the pragmatics of communication—and don't hear what their little subjects are saying. For an example of children failing to understand the experts, see Jean-Jacques Breton's (1993, 1995) demonstration that nine- to eleven-year-olds understand only 38 percent of the questions on the prestigious Diagnostic Interview Schedule for Children, an instrument used to diagnose psychiatric conditions in large populations of children.

4. Children Live in a Very Different World

Page 32: The first line of "The Fundamental Question of Metaphysics," the first chapter of Heidegger's *An Introduction to Metaphysics* (1961), reads "Why are there essents rather than nothing?" "Essents" are "existents," or simply "things that are" (page 1).

37: *"We've seen . . . absolutely normal children . . ."* People act in accordance with what they know. It's easy to dismiss the questions of children like Sam. It's far more difficult to dismiss the significance of the suicide of a man who received notification of another person's HIV status. Both the adult who killed himself and little Sam can reason only on the basis of the information currently available.

5. Logic, Experience, and Childhood Fears

Page 41: " 'To the eight-year-old . . .' " Bettelheim (1977).

42: "*. . . no child was ever interviewed more than once.*" Gruber and Vonèche (1977, pp. xxiv–xxv).

42–43: *"Here's a classic Piagetian interview . . ."* See Bringuier (1980, pp. 28–33) for the transcript of a fascinating interview between one of Piaget's assistants, Catherine Dami, and a six-year-old girl named Taïma. The exchange is about the conservation of substance—the fact that the amount doesn't change when a clay ball is rolled into a rope or stick and then back again into a ball. What is most striking about the interview is not the child's failure at a Piagetian developmental task, but that the child and the adult might just as well have been speaking two entirely different languages. (They were, actually—Kidspeak and Adultspeak.) Catherine Dami simply took for granted that the words and phrases she used had *exactly the same meaning* for little Taïma as they did for her, the adult. What we see is a beautiful exercise in miscommunication that is interpreted by Piaget as an equally beautiful illustration of his concepts. In fact, the whole exchange was an exercise in epistemological futility. The exchange is just as fascinating in French, where the disconnect between the adult and child worlds is strikingly illustrated by Dami's use of the informal *"tu"* form of address while little Taïma uses the formal *"vous"* (Bringuier 1977, pp. 52–53).

43: *"Well over half a century . . ."* Huang and Lee (1945). Not surprisingly, communication plays a big role in determining what kind of results researchers get. For example, the wording of questions can influence the correctness of the answer. "Does it have life?" was found to be more likely to elicit a correct response than "Is it alive?" (Klingensmith 1953). Similarly, *how* questions result in less magical and animistic explanations than *why* questions (Nass 1956). Children are also more likely to offer naturalistic explanations after manipulating the materials in question (Mogar 1960). Again, not surprisingly, children are more likely to offer naturalistic explanations when they watch a demonstration than when they are simply asked questions—illustrating the importance of context in children's understanding. All in all, Piaget went about his research in a manner entirely foreign to the cognitive-behavioral and communication styles of children. And it's not as if this data is new. Some of it, in fact, is well over a half century old! Margaret Mead pointed out as long ago as 1932 that animism is not an intrinsic feature of children's thinking and that children often reject the nonlogical magical concepts of adults (Mead 1932).

43–44: *"Realistic Child Development Research . . ."* See Margaret Donaldson's *Children's Minds* (Donaldson 1978) for a step-by-step account of how children succeed at classic Piagetian developmental tasks when they are made meaningful, understandable, and relevant. For Gelman, see Gelman (1978) and Gelman and Kremer (1991). For detailed treatment of children's *theory of mind*, see Astington (1993); Astington, Harris, et al. (1988); Harris (1989); and Wellman (1988, 1990). For the application of complex adaptive systems theory to child development, see Thelen (1989, 1992, 1996); Thelen and Smith (1994); and Smith and Thelen (1993). For Parsonson and Naughton's demonstration that children can not only master Piagetian "formal operations" at age five but also violate Piaget's "invariant sequence" of cognitive skill acquisition, see Parsonson and Naughton (1988).

45: *" 'One assumption' . . ."* Elkind (1976, p. 88). Elkind has played an important role in shaping child psychiatry's view of children's developmental capabilities (Elkind 1968, 1973, 1974, 1976, 1981, 1982).

46–47: *"What's a little mind supposed to do . . ."* Temple University mathematics professor John Allen Paulos notes in *Innumeracy* (Paulos 1988) that, simply on the basis of number, each year roughly sixty thousand Americans will have an accurate predictive dream solely by chance. As he stresses, while unlikely events are common in the world, they are extremely uncommon in the life of any given individual. So when an individual does experience an uncommon event, that experience can hit with tremendous psychological impact. And, as uncommon as unlikely events may be in the lives of any given individual, they tend to be very common in the lives of those who seek mental health treatment. All it takes is one unlikely event for a child or a family to cross the line between statistical normalcy and the horrendous or the bizarre.

For a brief review of the role of predictable and structuring experience in treating trauma, see Donovan (1991a and 1991b). For a detailed description of the role of experience in treating traumatized children, see Donovan and McIntyre (1990), especially "The Model of Inescapable Shock" (pp. 61–64) and "The Role of the Therapeutic Space in Modifying the Trauma Response" (pp. 139–43).

47–48: "Children's Experience of Space . . ." We were so struck by the fact that our colleagues seemed to take for granted that even the youngest of their child patients experience physical space and time exactly as they do that we began "The Therapeutic Space," chapter 6 of Healing the Hurt Child, with a reminder of how different that experience actually is. Many contemporary educators and therapists fail to realize that children's experience was very different in the pre-television, pre–video game world. Teachers and child therapists under forty-five or fifty years of age never knew that time when continents were far apart and natural catastrophic disasters and school shoot-outs were not something one could literally experience in Technicolor and Surround Sound right in one's own living room.

6. Pay Attention!

Page 53: "The significance of the fact . . ." Donovan (1996b, 1997).
54: "Besides what the computer world calls . . ." A more formal—but realistically nonpathologizing—description of dissociation:

Dissociation is a normative feature of human cognitive-behavioral style. As such, it refers to the fact that emotions, cognitive processes, and complex behavioral repertoires can be experienced and/or executed without conscious awareness on the part of the subject. In its most conceptually paradigmatic form, dissociation carries obvious evolutionary-adaptive value for it frees the organism from the adaptively dead-end necessity of attending consciously to every extero-/proprioceptive experience and evaluative and/or procedural decision, thereby permitting the organism to engage in simultaneous parallel autonomous or semi-autonomous multitasking behavior(s) in a variety of domains with a minimum of inter-task interference.

Dissociation allows for the partitioning of experience and agency within or between cognitive, affective, or kinesic domains. In its broadest sense, dissociation permits and facilitates the development and refinement of highly complex cognitive-behavioral skills and skill-repertoires including learning and social cognition, thereby permitting the subject to ignore-while-processing-and-acting-upon an immense and varied amount of internally- and externally-derived data (Donovan 1996b).

54:     *"We actually coined a term for such styles . . ."* We introduced this concept at the New Traumatology Conference, which we organized and cosponsored with the University of South Florida College of Medicine. See Donovan (1996b).

55:     *" 'Dissociative states are characterized by . . .' "* See Putnam (1989, pp. 6–8).

7. Now You Hear It, Now You Don't

Page 61:   *"There are two basic types of secrets . . ."* We first presented these ideas in very concentrated form in the chapter "Normative, Pathological and Therapeutic Dissociation" in *Healing the Hurt Child* (Donovan and McIntyre 1990, pp. 74–75).

8. How to Avoid the ADHD Trap by Using Communication to Shape Your Child's Attentional Style

Page 66:   *". . . something inherently wrong with Jack's brain . . ."* See Silver (1989) for a detailed enumeration of all the common childhood behaviors that the experts view as signs of attentional and learning disorders.

68:     *". . . life's extraordinary diversity . . ."* Unlike the cookie-cutter universal sameness model of children found in the education and mental health establishments, real life is nothing if not diverse! See Lewontin (1982) and Wilson (1992) for the work of two colleagues who disagree on a great deal—but not on diversity.

68:     *"Not only can this be done . . ."* Not only can naive mothers routinely modulate their babies' biobehavioral state with great sensitivity (Donovan 1997), so can dog breeders and trainers. For a wise, sensitive, realistic, respectful, and problem-solving approach to raising puppies, see *The Art of Raising a Puppy* by the Russian Orthodox Catholic Monks of New Skete (1991). The New Skete Brothers, whose monastic vocation is to breed and train German Shepherds, have a keen understanding of the temperament with which each pup is born and have developed very simple and practical techniques to assess it. Unlike most parents and child experts, however, the Monks of New Skete don't stop there. They don't just categorize puppies according to their categorical temperament and conclude that that's it for the dog's life. Instead, they have a keen understanding of how to capitalize on temperament as a strength upon which to build and they also realize how changeable basic temperament can be—if, that is, the trainer, just like the parent, is willing to take the time to understand these young creatures, their genuine capabilities, and their communication and relating styles. The monks also demonstrate a very practical understanding of the fundamental importance of structure, rules, and boundaries in raising and training a puppy as well as the paramount importance of consistency and continuity on the part of the trainer. It is a sad commentary on our contemporary society that very few parenting books—indeed, very few professional books about children—evidence the realistic understanding the Monks of New Skete have of dogs. (For a brief look at how far ahead the monks are of child psychiatry and the child/play psychotherapy field, see Donovan 1997b and 1997c.)

9. Who's in Charge Here?

Pages 84–85:
"... the 'healing power of play' ..." There are literally hundreds of thousands of child therapists in the world. The prevailing view in the child therapy/playtherapy field is that *play itself is curative* and that somehow children will heal themselves if they play in the presence of a child therapist. See Ablon (1996), Barnes (1996), Gil (1991), Gurney (1983), O'Connor (1991), Jernberg (1973a, 1973b), and Tanner and Mathis (1995).

10. "Choose to Be Your Real, Terrific, Good Self!"

Pages 103–5:
"*Actions Speak Louder Than Words*" See the section on "Parental Hypocrisy" in chapter 5 of *Healing the Hurt Child* (Donovan and McIntyre 1990, p. 97).

11. Mad, Bad, and Sad

Pages 111–12:
"*Our understanding of what anger is ...*" For the role of metaphor in human cognition, see Keller (1978, 1985); Lakoff (1972, 1987); Lakoff and Johnson (1980, 1998); and Johnson (1987).

116:
"*Integrative and Disintegrative Emotions*" For the integrative role of emotions, see Damasio (1994). We treat *sadness* rather differently than other writers. For example, Daniel Goleman in *Emotional Intelligence* (Daniel Goleman 1994) writes that "the main function for *sadness* is to help adjust to a significant loss, such as the death of someone close or a major disappointment." Goleman's definition of sadness makes it a totally *internal* phenomenon. We view and treat sadness as a social interpersonal phenomenon, a phenomenon that defines styles of reacting and relating. This makes it easier for us to help adults to recognize potential sadness—or when sadness would be appropriate—which, in turn, makes it easier for adults to change and modulate emotional and behavioral responses in themselves and in children.

12. Structure, Rules, and Boundaries

Page 136:
"*In a now-classic study ...*" Luke (1978). For several years, Luke's article went unnoticed by the medical profession. Today it is standard practice to check for bed-sharing in cases of sudden infant death syndrome.

14. Zero to Three, Bad Genes, and "Normal" Development

Pages
156–58:
"Should You Worry . . . ?" See Black and Greenough (1986), Black, Isaacs, et al. (1990), Donovan (1996a), Greenough (1987, 1996), Greenough and Black (1992), Greenough, Black, et al. (1991b).

158–62:
"Esther Thelen and her colleagues . . ." See Thelen (1984, 1989, 1992, 1995, 1996); Thelen and Smith (1994); and Thelen and Ulrich (1991).

160:
"Every year children who deviate from that supposedly straight developmental pathway . . ." James Lytle, adjunct professor of education at the University of Pennsylvania and chairman of the Council of Great Cities educational study, notes that if your child is staffed into "special" education—speech, hearing, and physical impairment excepted—he or she has only a 1.5 percent chance of *ever* returning to the mainstream as well as a much diminished likelihood of ever graduating from high school. Lytle (1988) and personal communication (1988). See also our discussion of these issues in Donovan and McIntyre (1990), pp. 172.

163:
"Stimulants have no positive effect . . ." Barkley and Cunningham (1979); Buhrmester, Whalen, et al. (1992); Charles and Schain (1981); and Swanson, Cantwell, et al. (1991, 1992). For the best reviews of the research, see Breggin (1998) and McGuinness (1989, 1995a, 1995b). Because stimulant medications "work" by damping the reorganizational potential of the brain, early "treatment" may foreclose all sorts of adaptive potential. See Sherman (1998) for the treatment, often with multiple medications, of Medicaid infants under age three—and even under twelve months of age. See Zito (1995) for the question of what effect decades of stimulant medication will have on developing brains.

163:
"Nobel laureate Richard Feynman . . ." See Gleick (1992, pp. 15–16, 25). Someone has doubtless already dubbed Richard Feynman one of the "LD men of eminence." After all, there was a massive discrepancy between his IQ and his academic achievement—the defining feature of a "learning disability." But nothing could be further from the truth. Feynman despised school and thought it a horribly barren, uninteresting "intellectual desert." Like another supposedly "learning-disabled" scientist—Thomas Edison, whose mother rescued him from an overbearing one-room schoolmaster in the third grade—Feynman didn't do well in school simply because he had better things to think about. And imagine the fate that would await Stephen Hawking, Lucasian Professor of Mathematics at Cambridge, a position once occupied by Sir Isaac Newton, if he rolled into school today! Wheelchair bound, unable to move, and lacking his speech synthesizer—he suffers from amyotrophic lateral sclerosis (ALS), a progressive deteriorating disease of the nervous system—Hawking would appear profoundly mentally retarded. Feynman's "development" improved as he aged; Hawking's worsened—yet at no point in their extraordinarily creative lives did their development reflect their true identity or their genuine potential.

164: *". . . Dr. Elizabeth M. Bryan notes . . ."* Bryan (1983, especially chapters 4–6).

166: *" 'We know that children . . .' "* Koplewicz (1996, p. 55).

168: *"Below is surely what has become . . ."* See Zametkin, Nordahl, et al. (1990).

169: *"The image itself is a favorite . . ."* The scientific establishment, the pharmaceutical companies, support groups, lobbying groups, government agencies, and funding sources are all intertwined and all quote and refer to one another. See Zametkin, Nordahl, et al. (1990) and Zametkin and Rapoport (1987) for the imaging material and AACAP (1997); Cantwell (1996); Koplewicz (1996); Hallowell and Ratey (1994); Phelen (1996); and Ratey and Johnson (1997) for the supposed significance of the images. Parents won't find any critical analysis in any of these sources.

169: *"Originally Lou, Henriksen, and Bruhn reported . . ."* See Lou, Henriksen, et al. (1984); Lou, Henriksen, et al. (1989).

169–70: *"So what should parents . . . conclude . . ."* See Hallowell and Ratey (1994) and Barkley (1995) for the claims and McGuinness (1989, 1995a, 1995b) for the critical analysis. See also AACAP (1997); Anonymous (1989); Lou (1984, 1989); and Wallis (1994).

170: *". . . 'the evidence is so equivocal . . .' "* See "Confidence Wanes in Search for Genetic Origins of Mental Illness," *The Psychiatric Times* (March 1989).

15. A Reminder for Teachers and Clinicians

Page 171: *". . . these abstractions are not actual children."* The most fundamental problem created by unrealistic approaches to childhood behavior problems is that they are—literally—not about children. See *Child and Adolescent Psychiatry: Modern Approaches* (Rutter and Hersov 1985) for a striking illustration. Although you will find over 1,700 references to the work of the senior editor in this famous text, you won't find a single child because there are no case histories to be found in its 960 pages—not even in the chapter "Individual and Group Psychotherapy."

172–74: Stevenson (1992a, 1992b); Stevenson, Chen, et al. (1993); and Stevenson and Stigler (1992).

172: *" '. . . but they have no vocabulary for them.' "* Harold Stevenson, personal communication, 1991.

173: *"Actually, American educators and . . ."* Tobin, Wu, and Davidson (1989).

173: *"As Merry White . . ."* White (1993).

173: *"Thus, for example, the current boom . . ."* See Ratey and Johnson (1997) for the new fad of "mild" psychiatric disorders.

173: *". . . the worst Japanese schools boast . . ."* Stevenson (1992a, 1992b); Stevenson, Chen, et al. (1993); and Stevenson and Stigler (1992).

174: *"Even eighth graders in those former Soviet bloc countries . . ."* See Bronner (1998).

176:    *"When a child like our third grader . . ."* See chapter 1 of *Healing the Hurt Child*
        (Donovan and McIntyre 1990) for a discussion of all the adult-style thinking
        and behavioral prerequisites a child must meet to qualify as a "candidate" for
        child psychotherapy.

176:    *"So look for these styles . . ."* See chapters 6 and 8 of this book and Donovan
        (1996b).

177:    " *'You Can't Help Me Until You Know What I Can't Do'* " Hodgins (1987).

178:    *"The Child Dissociative Checklist (CDC)"* Version 3.0 can be found in Put-
        nam (1997, appendix 2, pp. 354–60). The items on this checklist represent
        either normative childhood behaviors (which we view as eminently influ-
        enceable) or target behaviors to be challenged on the spot—not "develop-
        mental psychopathology" to be documented and treated over months
        or years.

179:    *"Often, when we do workshops . . ."* See "The Therapeutic Space," pp.
        110–43 in Donovan and McIntyre (1990).

181:    For Freud's views on how children conceive of death, see Freud (1953/1900,
        p. 254).

Appendix: Parents Ask About the Five Minutes

Page 186:   For the special challenges posed by twins, see Bryan (1983, 1984).

Bibliography

Ablon, S. L. (1996). "The therapeutic action of play." *Journal of the American Academy of Child and Adolescent Psychiatry* 35(4): 545–47.

Adams, P., and I. Fras (1988). *Beginning Child Psychiatry*. New York, Brunner/Mazel.

American Academy of Child and Adolescent Psychiatry (1997). "Practice Parameters for the Assessment and Treatment of Children and Adolescents with Attention-Deficit/Hyperactivity Disorder of the AACAP" @www.aacap.org/members only. Washington, D.C., American Academy of Child and Adolescent Psychiatry.

American Psychiatric Association (1987). *Diagnostic and Statistical Manual, Third Edition (Revised)*. Washington, D.C., American Psychiatric Association.

Andreason, N. C. (1984). *The Broken Brain: The Biological Revolution in Psychiatry*. New York, Harper & Row.

Anonymous (1989). "Confidence Wanes in Search for Genetic Origins of Mental Illness." *Psychiatric Times*, March.

Astington, J. W. (1993). *The Child's Discovery of the Mind*. Cambridge, Mass., Harvard University Press.

Astington, J. W., P. L. Harris, et al., eds. (1988). *Developing Theories of Mind*. New York, Cambridge University Press.

Barkley, R. A. (1995). *Taking Charge of ADHD: The Complete Authoritative Guide for Parents*. New York, Guilford Press.

Barkley, R. A., and C. E. Cunningham (1979). "Stimulant drugs and activity level in hyperactive children." *American Journal of Orthopsychiatry* 49(3): 491–99.

Barnes, M. (1996). *The Healing Path with Children: An Exploration for Parents and Professionals*. No location specified, Viktoria, Fermoyle & Berrigan Publishing.

Bettelheim, B. (1977). *The Uses of Enchantment: The Meaning and Importance of Fairy Tales*. New York, Vintage Books.

Black, J. E., and W. T. Greenough (1986). "Induction of pattern in neural structure by experience: Implications for cognitive development." In *Advances in Developmental*

Psychology. Vol. 4, edited by M. E. Lamb, A. L. Brown, and B. Rogoff, 1–50. Hillsdale, N.J., Erlbaum.

Black, J. E., K. R. Isaacs, et al. (1990). "Learning causes synaptogenesis, while motor activity causes angiogenesis, in cerebellar cortex of adult rats." *Proceedings of the National Academy of Sciences* 87: 5568–72.

Brainerd, C. J. (1973a). "Judgments and explanations as criteria for the presence of cognitive structure." *Psychological Bulletin* 79:172–79.

———(1973b). "Neo-Piagetian training experiments revisited: Is there any support for the cognitive-developmental stage hypothesis?" *Cognition* 2:349–70.

———(1974). "The concept of structure in cognitive-developmental theory." Paper presented at the annual convention of the American Psychological Association, New Orleans, La.

———(1977). "Response criteria in concept development research." *Child Development* 48:60–366.

———(1978). "The stage question in cognitive-developmental theory." *Behavioral and Brain Sciences* 2:1173–213.

Breggin, P. R. (1998). *Talking Back to Ritalin: What Doctors Aren't Telling You About Stimulants for Children*. Monroe, Maine, Common Courage Press.

Breton, J.-J., L. Bergeron, et al. (1993). "Do children aged 9 to 11 understand questions from the DISC-2?" Paper presented at the annual meeting of the American Academy of Child and Adolescent Psychiatry, San Antonio, Tex.

———(1995). "Do children aged 9 to 11 understand the DISC Version 2.25 questions?" *Journal of the American Academy of Child and Adolescent Psychiatry* 34(7):946–54.

Bringuier, J.-C. (1977). *Conversations libres avec Jean Piaget*. Paris, Éditions Robert Laffont.

———(1980). *Conversations with Jean Piaget*. Chicago, University of Chicago Press.

Bronner, E. (1998). "U.S. high school seniors among worst in math and science." *The New York Times*, February 25:A3–11.

Bryan, E. M. (1983). *The Nature and Nurture of Twins*. London, Ballière Tindall.

———(1984). *Twins in the Family: A Parent's Guide*. London, Constable.

Buhrmester, D., C. K. Whalen, et al. (1992). "Prosocial behavior in hyperactive boys: Effects of stimulant medication and comparison with normal boys." *Journal of Abnormal Child Psychology* 20(1):103–21.

Cantwell, D. P. (1996). "Attention Deficit Disorder: A review of the last 10 years." *Journal of the American Academy of Child and Adolescent Psychiatry* 35(8):978–87.

Cantwell, D., and L. Baker (1987). *Developmental Speech and Language Disorders*. New York, Guilford Press.

Changeux, J.-P. (1985). *Neuronal Man*. New York, Pantheon.

Charles, L., and R. Schain (1981). "A four-year follow-up study of the effects of methylphenidate on the behavior and academic achievement of hyperactive children." *Journal of Abnormal Child Psychology* 9(4):495–505.

Damasio, A. R. (1994). *Descartes' Error: Emotion, Reason, and the Human Brain*. New York, Grosset/Putnam.

Davies, P., ed. (1989). *The New Physics*. New York, Cambridge University Press.

Donaldson, M. (1978). *Children's Minds*. New York, W. W. Norton.

Donovan, D. M. (1991a). "The disappearance of the child from child psychiatry." Grand Rounds, Department of Psychiatry, National Children's Medical Center, Washington, D.C., December 13, 1991.

———(1991b). "Traumatology: A field whose time has come." *Journal of Traumatic Stress* 4(3): 433–36.

———(1992). "Traumatology: What's in a name?" *Journal of Traumatic Stress* 6(3):409–12.

———(1996a). "A new model for 21st century traumatology: Why the field needs the greenoughs and thelens of Science." Paper presented at the New Traumatology Conference, Clearwater Beach, Fla.

———(1996b). "A new model of dissociation and dissociogenesis: Putting the child back into 'childhood antecedents.' " Plenary address delivered at the New Traumatology Conference, Clearwater Beach, Fla.

———(1997a). "Why memory is a red herring in the recovered (traumatic) memory debate." In *Recollections of Trauma: Scientific Evidence and Clinical Practice*, edited by J. D. Read and D. S. Lindsay, 403–15. New York, Plenum Press.

———(1997b). "Letter: The play therapy controversy—Therapeutic play." *Journal of the American Academy of Child and Adolescent Psychiatry* 36(1):3–4.

——— (1997c). "Letter: The play therapy controversy continues." *Journal of the American Academy of Child and Adolescent Psychiatry* 36(10):1322–33.

Donovan, D. M., and D. McIntyre (1990). *Healing the Hurt Child: A Developmental-Contextual Approach*. New York, W. W. Norton.

Elkind, D. (1968). "Jean Piaget: Giant in the nursery." *New York Times Magazine* 6 (May 26):27–32.

———(1970). *Children and Adolescents: Interpretive Essays on Jean Piaget*. New York, Oxford University Press.

———(1973). Measuring young minds: An introduction to the ideas of Jean Piaget. In *Jean Piaget: The Man and His Ideas*, edited by R. I. Evans. New York, Dutton.

———(1974). *Children and Adolescents: Interpretive Essays on Jean Piaget*. New York, Oxford University Press.

———(1976). *Child Development and Education: A Piagetian Perspective*. New York, Oxford University Press.

———(1981). "Child development research and early childhood education." *Young Children* 1:2–9.

———(1982). "Piagetian psychology and the practice of child psychiatry." *Journal of the American Academy of Child and Adolescent Psychiatry* 21(5):435–45.

Freud, S. (1953/1900). *The Interpretation of Dreams*. London, Hogarth Press.

Gelman, R. (1978). "Cognitive development." *Annual Review of Psychology* 29:297–332.

Gelman, S. A., and K. E. Kremer (1991). "Understanding natural cause: Children's explanations of how objects and their properties originate." *Child Development* 62(2):396–414.

Gil, E. (1991). *The Healing Power of Play: Working with Abused Children*. New York, Guilford Press.

Gleick, J. (1987). *Chaos: Making a New Science*. New York, Penguin.

———(1992). *Genius: The Life and Science of Richard Feynman*. New York, Pantheon.

Goleman, D. (1994). *Emotional Intelligence: Why It Can Matter More Than IQ*. New York, Bantam.

Greenough, W. T. (1987). "Experience and brain development." *Child Development*, 58:539–59.

———(1996). "A history of neuroplasticity research." Paper presented at the New Traumatology Conference, Clearwater Beach, Fla.

Greenough, W. T., and B. J. Anderson (1991). "Cerebellar synaptic plasticity: Relation to learning versus neural activity." In *Activity-Driven CNS Changes in Learning and Development*, edited by J. R. Wolpaw, J. T. Schmidt, and T. M. Vaughan, 627. New York, New York Academy of Sciences.

Greenough, W. T., and J. E. Black (1992). "Induction of brain structure by experience: Substrates for cognitive development." In *Developmental Behavioral Neuroscience*, edited by M. Gunnar and C. Nelson, 155–200. Hillsdale, N.J., Erlbaum.

Greenough, W. T., J. E. Black, et al. (1991). "Experience and brain development." *Child Development* 58:539–59.

Gruber, H. E., and J.-J. Vonèche, eds. (1977). *The Essential Piaget*. New York, Basic Books.

Gurney, L. (1983). "Client-centered (nondirective) play therapy." In *Handbook of Play Therapy*, edited by C. E. Schaefer and K. L. O'Connor, 21–64. New York, Wiley.

Hallowell, E. M., and J. J. Ratey (1994). *Driven to Distraction: Recognizing and Coping with Attention Deficit Disorder from Childhood Through Adulthood*. New York, Random House.

Harris, P. L. (1989). *Children and Emotion: The Development of Psychological Understanding*. Oxford, Basil Blackwell.

Heidegger, M. (1961). *An Introduction to Metaphysics*. New York, Pantheon.

Hodgins, D. (1987). "You can't help me until you know what I can't do." Paper presented at the annual meeting of the National Association for the Education of Young Children, Chicago.

Horgan, J. (1993). "The new eugenics." *Scientific American* 286(6):123–31.

Huang, I., and H. W. Lee (1945). "Experimental analysis of child animism." *Journal of Genetic Psychology* 66:69–74.

Hubel, D. H., and T. Wiesel (1962). "Receptive fields binocular interaction and functional architecture in the cat's visual cortex." *Journal of Physiology* (London) 160:106–54.

Jernberg, A. (1973a). "Theraplay technique." In *The Therapeutic Use of Child's Play*, edited by C. Schaefer. New York, Aronson.

———(1973b). *Theraplay*. San Francisco, Jossey-Bass.

Johnson, M. (1987). *The Body in the Mind: The Bodily Basis of Meaning, Imagination, and Reason*. Chicago, University of Chicago Press.

Keller, E. F. (1978). "Gender and Science." *Psychoanalysis and Contemporary Thought* 1:409–33.

———(1985). *Reflections on Gender and Science*. New Haven, Conn., Yale University Press.

Klingensmith, S. W. (1953). "Child animism: What the child means by 'alive.'" *Child Development* 24:51–61.

Koplewicz, H. S. (1996). *It's Nobody's Fault: New Hope and Help for Difficult Children and Their Parents*. New York, Times Books/Random House.

Kotulak, R. (1996). *Inside the Brain: Revolutionary Discoveries of How the Mind Works.* Kansas City, Mo., Andrews, McMeel.

Lakoff, G. (1972). "Hedges: A study in meaning criteria and the logic of fuzzy concepts." In *Papers from the Eighth Regional Meeting,* Chicago Linguistic Society.

———(1987). *Women, Fire and Dangerous Things: What Categories Reveal About the Mind.* Chicago, University of Chicago Press.

———(1990). "The Invariance hypothesis: Is abstract reason based on image schemas?" *Cognitive Linguistics* 1:39–74.

Lakoff, G., and M. Johnson (1980). *Metaphors We Live By.* Chicago, University of Chicago Press.

———(1998). *Philosophy in the Flesh: The Embodied Mind and Its Challenge to Western Thought.* New York, Basic Books.

Lewontin, R. C. (1982). *Human Diversity.* San Francisco, Scientific American Books.

Lou, H. C., L. Henriksen, et al. (1984). "Focal cerebral hypoperfusion in children with dysphasia and/or attention deficit disorder." *Archives of Neurology* 41:825–29.

———(1989). "Striatal dysfunction in attention deficit and hyperkinetic disorder." *Archives of Neurology* 46:48–52.

Luke, J. L. (1978). "Sleeping arrangements of sudden infant death syndrome victims in the District of Columbia—A preliminary report." *Journal of Forensic Sciences* 23(2):279–383.

Matthews, G. B. (1980). *Philosophy and the Young Child.* Cambridge, Mass., Harvard University Press.

McGuinness, D. (1989). "Attention deficit disorder: The emperor's clothes, animal 'pharm,' and other fiction." In *The Limits of Biological Treatments for Psychological Distress: Comparisons with Psychotherapy and Placebo,* edited by S. Fisher and R. Greenberg, 151–87. Hillsdale, N.J., Erlbaum.

———(1995a). "Ritalin and the cocaine connection: The impact of methylphenidate on the central and peripheral nervous system. Part I: Animal research." University of South Florida, unpublished manuscript.

———(1995b). "Ritalin and the cocaine connection: The impact of methylphenidate on the central and peripheral nervous system. Part II: Human research." University of South Florida, unpublished manuscript.

Mead, M. (1932). "An investigation of the thought of primitive children, with special reference to animism." *Journal of the Royal Anthropological Institute* 62:173–90.

Modgil, S., and C. Modgil (1982). *The Taming of Piaget: Crossfires and Crosscurrents.* London, National Foundation for Research.

Mogar, M. (1960). "Children's causal reasoning about natural phenomena." *Child Development* 31:59–65.

Monks of New Skete, The (1991). *The Art of Raising a Puppy.* New York, Little, Brown.

Nash, J. M. (1997). "Fertile minds." *Time,* February 19:149.

Nass, M. L. (1956). "The effects of three variables on children's concepts of physical causality." *Abnormal Social Psychology* 53:191–96.

O'Connor, K. J. (1991). *The Play Therapy Primer: An Integration of Theories and Techniques.* New York, Wiley-Interscience.

Parsonson, B. S., and K. A. Naughton (1988). "Training generalized conservation in 5–year-old children." *Journal of Experimental Child Psychology* 46:372–90.

Paulos, J. A. (1988). *Innumeracy: Mathematical Illiteracy and Its Consequences*. New York, Hill and Wang.

Phelen, T. W. (1996). *All About Attention Deficit Disorder*. Glen Ellyn, Ill., Child Management, Inc.

Putnam, F. W. (1989). *Diagnosis and Treatment of Multiple Personality Disorder*. New York, Guilford Press.

———(1997). *Dissociation in Children and Adolescents: A Developmental Perspective*. New York, Guilford Press.

Ratey, J. J., and C. Johnson (1997). *Shadow Syndromes*. New York, Pantheon.

Rutter, M., and L. Hersov, eds. (1985). *Child and Adolescent Psychiatry: Modern Approaches*. Oxford, Blackwell.

Saussure, F. de (1972–1916). *Course in General Linguistics*. La Salle, Ill., Open Court.

Sherman, C. (1998). "Some Michigan Medicaid babies treated for ADHD." *Clinical Psychiatry News* 26(7):6–7.

Siegel, L. S., and C. J. Brainerd, eds. (1978). *Alternatives to Piaget*. New York, Academic Press.

Silver, L. B. (1989). "Psychological and family problems associated with learning disabilities: Assessment and intervention." *Journal of the American Academy of Child and Adolescent Psychiatry* 28(3):319–25.

Smith, F., and J. H. Dougherty (1965). "Natural phenomena as explained by children." *Journal of Educational Research* 59:137–40.

Smith, L. B., and E. Thelen (1993). *A Dynamic Systems Approach to Development: Applications*. Cambridge, Mass., MIT Press.

Spitzer, R. (1989). *DSM-III-R Casebook—A Learning Companion to the Diagnostic and Statistical Manual of Mental Disorders, Third Edition, Revised*. Washington, D.C., American Psychiatric Press.

Stevenson, H. W. (1992a). "Learning from Asian schools." *Scientific American* 276(6):70–76.

———(1992b). "Con: Don't deceive children through a feel-good approach." (R. W. Reasoner, executive director, California Center for Self-Esteem, Mountain View, Calif. "Pro: You can bring hope to failing students.") *The School Administrator* April: 23, 25, 27, 30.

Stevenson, H. W., C. Chen, et al. (1993). "Mathematics achievement of Chinese, Japanese, and American children: Ten years later. *Science* 259(January 1):52–58.

Stevenson, H. W., and J. W. Stigler (1992). *The Learning Gap: Why Our Schools Are Failing and What We Can Learn from Japanese and Chinese Education*. New York, Summit Books.

Swanson, J. M., D. Cantwell, et al. (1991). "Effects of stimulant medication on learning in children with ADHD." *Journal of Learning Disabilities* 24:219–27.

———(1992). "Treatment of ADHD: Beyond medication." *Beyond Behavior* 4(1):13–22.

Tanner, Z., and R. D. Mathis (1995). "A child-centered typology for training novice play therapists." *International Journal of Play Therapy* 4(2):1–13.

Thelen, E. (1984). "Learning to walk: Ecological determinants and psychological constraints." In *Advances in Infancy Research*, edited by L. Lipsitt and C. Rovee-Collier,
3. Norwood, N.J., Ablex.

———(1989). "Self-organization in developmental processes." In *Systems and Development*, edited by M. Gunnar and E. Thelen. Hillsdale, N.J., Erlbaum.

———(1992). "Development as a dynamic system." *Current Directions in Psychological Science* 6:189–93.

———(1995). "Motor development: A new synthesis." *American Psychologist*
50(2):79–95.

———(1996). "A complex adaptive systems approach to the development of cognition
and action." Paper delivered at the New Traumatology Conference, Clearwater
Beach, Fla.

Thelen, E., and L. S. Smith (1994). *A Dynamic Systems Approach to the Development of
Cognition and Action*. Cambridge, Mass., MIT Press.

Thelen, E., and B. D. Ulrich (1991). "Hidden skills: A dynamic analysis of treadmill step-
ping during the first year." *Monographs of the Society for Research in Child Development*
(Serial No. 223) 56(1).

Tobin, J. J., D. Y. H. Wu, D. H. Davidson (1989). *Preschool in Three Cultures: China, Japan
and the United States*. New Haven, Conn., Yale University Press.

Volkow, N. D., Y. Ding, J. S. Fowler, et al. (1995). "Is methylphenidate like cocaine?"
Archives of General Psychiatry 52:456–63.

Waldrop, M. M. (1992). *Complexity: The Emerging Science at the Edge of Order and Chaos*.
New York, Simon & Schuster.

Wallis, C. (1994). "Life in overdrive." *Newsweek*, July 18:44–50.

Wellman, H. M. (1985). "The child's theory of mind: The development of conceptions of
cognition." In *The Growth of Reflection*, edited by S. R. Yussen, 169–206. New York,
Academic Press.

———(1988). "First steps in the child's theorizing about the mind." In *Developing Theories of Mind*, edited by J. W. Astington, P. L. Harris, and D. R. Olson. New York, Cambridge University Press.

———(1990). *The Child's Theory of the Mind*. Cambridge, Mass., MIT Press.

White, M. (1993). *The Material Child: Coming of Age in Japan and America*. New York,
Free Press.

Wilson, E. O. (1992). *The Diversity of Life*. New York, W. W. Norton.

Wingert, P., and B. Kantrowitz (1997). "Why Andy couldn't read." *Newsweek*, October
27:56–64.

Zametkin, A. J., T. E. Nordahl, et al. (1990). "Cerebral glucose metabolism in adults with
hyperactivity of childhood onset." *New England Journal of Medicine* 323:1361–67.

Zametkin, A. J., and J. L. Rapoport (1987). "Neurobiology of attention deficit disorder
with hyperactivity: Where have we come in 50 years?" *Journal of the American
Academy of Child and Adolescent Psychiatry* 26:676–86.

Zito, J. M. (1995). "Pharmacoepidemiology meets epidemiology." *Newsletter of the American Academy of Child and Adolescent Psychiatry* July-August: 32, 34.

Acknowledgments

We owe very special thanks to Ronni Parker and Anne Sullivan for their constant encouragement over the years and for their patient reminders that it was parents, not professionals, who would be most likely to hear what we had to say—and to Michael May, whose kindness and moral support were sweetness in difficult times.

We also want to thank Barbara Bradbury, David Butler, Marienne Dierking-Reese, Christine Evans, Paul J. Evans, Sidney Goetz, Miriam Toll Goetz, Betty Gorman, Sarah Gorman, Myrna Johnson, Donna Jo Leake, Julie McNichols, Ann Motten, Matthew Parker, Amy Smith, Melinda Techler, Richard Theriault, Merry White, and Kim Whitener for their comments on the manuscript in its various stages of completion, and William Silverstein for the "walking" illustrations in chapter 14. We owe Chris Noto special thanks for alerting us to the fact that Bill Watterson is a kindred spirit and that we would do well to let Calvin do some of the talking.

We owe a special debt of gratitude to Diane McGuinness, without whom we might never have discovered our marvelous agent, Jennie McDonald of Curtis Brown, Ltd., who not only believed in the value of what we had to say but also patiently guided the crafting of a long and complex proposal to successful completion. Finally, perhaps our biggest debt of gratitude goes to William Patrick, our first editor at Henry Holt and Company, whose vision, understanding, patience, and superb editorial skills not only made *What Did I Just Say!?!* a much better book, but also provided a living lesson in good writing.

All the above notwithstanding, we are really most indebted to the many parents and children with whom we have worked over the years and who have taught us so much.

Index

Italic page numbers refer to illustrations.